The Sustainability Revolution

By Adam Robeck

Table of contents

Introduction

The world today stands at a crossroads—on one side lies the possibility of a sustainable future, a thriving planet where ecosystems are restored, carbon emissions are reduced, and natural resources are used responsibly. On the other side is a grim reality shaped by decades of environmental degradation: rising global temperatures, the relentless destruction of habitats, collapsing biodiversity, and mounting pollution. The choice before us is stark, and the stakes have never been higher.

As we enter the 21st century, the environmental challenges facing our planet are both unprecedented and deeply interconnected. The climate crisis looms large, with atmospheric carbon levels higher than at any time in human history, driving extreme weather patterns, melting ice caps, and rising sea levels. These changes are not abstract or distant; they are already reshaping our world, from devastating wildfires in California and Australia to catastrophic flooding in Pakistan, to heatwaves across Europe. Extreme weather events, once considered rare, have become regular occurrences, threatening lives, economies, and entire ecosystems.

At the same time, our planet's biodiversity is in freefall. Species are disappearing at an alarming rate—faster than at any point since the extinction of the dinosaurs. According to the United Nations, up to one million species face the threat of extinction, driven by habitat loss, overexploitation, pollution, and climate change. The loss of these species isn't just an ecological tragedy; it's a profound blow to the resilience of the ecosystems that sustain us, including pollinators that are critical to food production and forests that act as carbon sinks. In fact, the extinction of even a single species can set off a chain reaction, disturbing entire ecosystems and threatening the survival of other species, including humans.

Pollution—both visible and invisible—further exacerbates our environmental plight. Plastic waste has become a ubiquitous presence in our oceans, rivers, and landscapes. It is estimated that over 8 million tons of plastic enter the oceans every year, suffocating marine life and poisoning the food chain. Meanwhile, the air we breathe is increasingly toxic, with pollution levels in cities around the world reaching hazardous levels, contributing to respiratory diseases, cardiovascular problems, and premature deaths. Our oceans, once pristine, now harbor vast "dead zones," areas of water so devoid of oxygen that most marine life cannot survive. This pollution is not only a threat to wildlife but also to the health of communities, particularly those in low-income and marginalized areas, who often bear the brunt of environmental degradation.

The water crisis is another critical challenge. With roughly two-thirds of the global population experiencing water scarcity at least one month of the year, access to clean and safe water is becoming an increasingly rare commodity. Groundwater depletion, pollution of freshwater sources, and climate-driven changes in precipitation patterns are all contributing to the growing water stress in many parts of the world. In cities like Cape Town, South Africa, residents have faced the very real threat of running out of water altogether. Meanwhile, in places like India, millions still live without access to safe drinking water, while aquifers that have sustained agriculture for generations are rapidly drying up.

Our unsustainable consumption of natural resources and the destruction of vital ecosystems are eroding the very foundations of life on Earth. Deforestation continues to ravage the Amazon, the Congo Basin, and Southeast Asia, while industrial agriculture clears vast tracts of land for monoculture crops, further contributing to soil degradation, water contamination, and loss of biodiversity. The insatiable demand for timber, palm oil, beef, and other commodities has transformed forests into commodity pipelines, threatening the delicate balance of the natural world.

These environmental crises are not isolated; they are deeply interwoven, each one amplifying the other. Climate change accelerates deforestation, while pollution fuels the extinction of species. Droughts and water scarcity are exacerbated by the loss of forests and wetlands, which play a crucial role in water retention and regulation. In turn, the depletion of natural resources and the destruction of ecosystems undermine the very services upon which human life depends: food, clean water, breathable air, and a stable climate.

At the heart of these crises lies a model of development that prioritizes short-term profit over long-term sustainability. Driven by corporate greed, unchecked industrial expansion, and a consumer culture built on excess, this model has led us to a point where the planet's natural systems are no longer able to bear the weight of human activity. In a world where economic growth is often equated with environmental harm, we face a paradox: the very systems that have driven progress have also created the conditions for the crisis we now face.

The clock is ticking. We are living in a moment where the consequences of our actions, or inaction, will reverberate for generations. Environmental degradation is no longer a distant possibility—it is a present-day reality, unfolding before our eyes. The urgency of addressing these issues cannot be overstated. If we fail to act decisively, we risk leaving behind a world that is less hospitable, less livable, and less capable of supporting the biodiversity and ecosystems that sustain life on Earth.

Scientific evidence makes it clear: we are on a trajectory toward irreversible damage. Global temperatures have already risen by approximately 1.2°C since the pre-industrial era, and we are on track to surpass 1.5°C by as early as 2030. This seemingly modest increase in temperature is already wreaking havoc on the planet. In many regions, we're seeing heatwaves that break records year after year, wildfires that rage with unprecedented ferocity, and glaciers and ice sheets that are melting at rates faster than previously predicted. Each fraction of a degree matters, as the intensity and frequency of extreme weather events increase.

As temperatures rise, so does the frequency of extreme weather events—hurricanes, floods, droughts, and heatwaves—that devastate communities, economies, and ecosystems. The impacts are disproportionately felt by vulnerable populations—particularly those in developing nations, indigenous communities, and lower-income areas. In 2020 alone, climate-related disasters caused more than $210 billion in damages globally. But the true cost is immeasurable: lives lost, livelihoods destroyed, and entire ecosystems rendered uninhabitable.

While much of the focus has been on climate change, we must recognize that biodiversity loss is just as urgent, if not more so. The extinction rate today is 1,000 times higher than the natural background rate, and it continues to rise. The World Economic Forum has identified biodiversity loss as one of the top global risks. The destruction of rainforests, coral reefs, and wetlands is not just an ecological issue—it's a crisis that jeopardizes food security, medicine, clean water, and the very air we breathe. Insects, which play critical roles in pollination, soil aeration, and decomposition, are disappearing at alarming rates. Pollinators like bees and butterflies, which are vital for agriculture, are in steep decline. This spells disaster for global food production, which relies heavily on these species. Insects are responsible for 35% of the world's food production, yet the decline of insect populations is projected to result in catastrophic losses in food security.

The urgency of addressing these crises is compounded by pollution. The chemicals and plastics we produce are suffocating our oceans, poisoning the air we breathe, and contaminating freshwater supplies. The oceans, once considered vast and resilient, are now suffused with toxic chemicals and plastic waste. Over 8 million tons of plastic enter the ocean every year, leading to the creation of massive "garbage patches" in the Pacific, Atlantic, and Indian Oceans. Marine life is ingesting this plastic, often fatally. And as plastics break down, they release harmful chemicals into the water, disrupting marine ecosystems and contaminating the food chain. Similarly, air pollution has become a global health crisis, contributing to millions of premature deaths each year, particularly in urban areas. The burning of fossil fuels, industrial emissions, and agricultural practices release particulate matter and toxic gases that cause respiratory diseases, cardiovascular problems, and cancer. In some cities, air quality is so poor that the risk of disease from pollution is greater than from tobacco smoking.

Water scarcity is a silent but equally pressing issue. By 2025, it is estimated that two-thirds of the world's population could face water shortages. Droughts in regions like California, parts of Africa, and South Asia are worsening, and the depletion of groundwater reserves has reached alarming levels. In many areas, competition for water is intensifying, not only for agricultural use but also for consumption by growing urban populations. Rivers are drying up, and aquifers that have taken centuries to replenish are being depleted at unsustainable rates. The impact of this scarcity will be felt in food production, health outcomes, and geopolitical stability. Water is the lifeblood of our planet—without it, nothing survives.

At the heart of this urgency lies a fundamental conflict: the disconnect between economic growth and environmental preservation. For decades, we have subscribed to a model of development that prioritizes economic expansion over ecological stability. The relentless extraction of natural resources—oil, gas, minerals, timber, water—has been central to the world's economic engine. However, this model is unsustainable. It has led to the overconsumption of resources at a pace that exceeds the Earth's capacity to regenerate. The planet's ecological limits are being pushed beyond their breaking point. As we continue to extract resources, degrade ecosystems, and emit pollutants into the air, land, and water, we are destabilizing the very systems that support life. If we do not change course, we will find ourselves on a trajectory that leads to irreversible damage to the climate, ecosystems, and human health.

The consequences of continuing with business as usual are stark. By the end of the century, if we continue to ignore the signs, sea levels could rise by more than 3 feet (1 meter), displacing millions of people and flooding coastal cities. Forests could be reduced to barren land, leaving no habitat for wildlife and no natural carbon sink to combat rising emissions. Freshwater scarcity could trigger conflicts over water rights, food shortages, and mass migrations. Our food systems could collapse, as agriculture becomes more difficult and less predictable, with crop failures due to droughts, floods, and changing weather patterns.

However, there is still hope—but only if we act swiftly and decisively. The window of opportunity to prevent the most catastrophic effects of these crises is closing, but it is not yet closed. Every year of delay makes the task more difficult, but every action we take can still mitigate the worst outcomes. The actions we take today—whether in the form of cutting emissions, restoring ecosystems, investing in renewable energy, or enacting meaningful policies—will have a profound impact on the future we leave behind. The future is not predetermined; it is something we can shape, but only if we act with the urgency and commitment that the crises demand.

The time for half-measures and slow progress is over. We need bold, transformative action, not just from governments and corporations, but from all sectors of society. The magnitude of the challenge is daunting, but so is the potential for change. This is the moment we have been waiting for: a turning point where we must decide whether we want to continue down the destructive path we are on, or whether we will rise to the occasion and fight for a planet that can sustain future generations.

We stand at a critical juncture, and the choice is ours. The climate crisis, the rapid loss of biodiversity, pollution, and the depletion of our natural resources are not problems for the distant future—they are here, right now, and they demand our immediate attention. Yet, despite the overwhelming evidence, the solutions we need to address these crises have too often been delayed, distorted, or dismissed by those in power. Whether it's through corporate lobbying, political inaction, or misinformation, the forces resisting change are formidable. But the time for complacency has passed.

This is where you come in. While systemic change requires the mobilization of governments, corporations, and international bodies, we cannot wait for others to act. Each of us, as individuals, has the power to make a meaningful difference. The choices we make in our everyday lives—the products we buy, the energy we use, the food we consume, and the policies we support—can have a profound impact on the environment. But action must extend beyond our personal consumption. Collective action, grassroots movements, and demands for stronger legislation can shift the tides of change. The pressure to hold corporations accountable for environmental harm, to demand political leaders enact stronger policies, and to invest in renewable energy and sustainable technologies must come from all of us. Every voice counts.

This book is a call to arms for those who understand that the future of the planet is at stake. But it's not a call to despair; it's a rallying cry to engage, to act, and to be part of the solution. Whether you are a policymaker, a business leader, a concerned citizen, or someone just beginning to explore these issues, there is work to be done—and there is hope. Solutions are not only possible, they are already within reach. They exist in the innovations of renewable energy, the regenerative power of sustainable farming, the ingenuity of circular economies, and the tireless efforts of grassroots activists who are transforming their communities and the world. By making conscious, informed decisions today, we can protect and restore the planet for the generations that will follow.

The urgency is real. But so too is the power we hold to make a difference. Every action, no matter how small, contributes to the larger movement toward environmental sustainability. Together, we can combat corporate greed, dismantle the systems that have long been designed to exploit the Earth, and build a future that is healthier, more just, and more sustainable.

The path ahead is challenging, but it is also brimming with opportunity. We are living in a moment where history is being written—and the choices we make today will determine the legacy we leave for future generations. The environmental crises we face are urgent and interconnected, but they are not insurmountable. Through innovation, education, political will, and collective action, we can still turn the tide.

In the chapters that follow, we will explore the complexity of these challenges, highlight the profound impact they are already having on the planet and its inhabitants, and provide a blueprint for the transformative actions we must take. We will shine a light on the forces that stand in the way of progress—corporate interests, political obstruction, and misinformation—and expose the power dynamics that keep us stuck in a cycle of environmental destruction. But we will also celebrate the solutions that exist, from grassroots activism to cutting-edge technologies, and the individuals and communities driving these changes.

This is not just a book about problems; it is a book about solutions. It is a roadmap for those who are ready to take bold action and fight for a sustainable future. The time to act is now—our planet cannot afford to wait any longer. It's up to all of us to rise to the challenge, embrace our responsibility, and ensure that future generations inherit a world that is capable of thriving, not just surviving. The call to action is clear: we must act, and we must act together.

Chapter 1

The Pressing Global Environmental Issues

The environmental challenges we face today are nothing short of monumental. From the rapid acceleration of climate change to the widespread collapse of ecosystems, the signs of distress are visible everywhere. While the impacts of these crises may appear distant or abstract to some, they are already reshaping our world in tangible, often devastating ways. If we are to secure a livable planet for future generations, we must first understand the full scope of the environmental issues we face.

Climate Change: The Global Temperature Crisis

At the heart of today's environmental crises lies climate change, the most profound and far-reaching challenge humanity has ever faced. The scientific consensus is clear: human activity—particularly the burning of fossil fuels (coal, oil, and natural gas), deforestation, and industrial agriculture—is driving a rapid and dangerous increase in global temperatures. Since the start of the Industrial Revolution in the 18th century, the Earth has warmed by approximately 1.2°C (2.2°F). While this might seem like a small increase, it is already having catastrophic effects on the planet. The trajectory we are on suggests that we are headed for a rise in temperatures of 3°C (5.4°F) or more by the end of the century if no meaningful action is taken.

The Greenhouse Effect and Its Amplification

The Earth's climate operates through a natural process called the greenhouse effect, where certain gases in the atmosphere, such as carbon dioxide (CO_2), methane (CH_4), and nitrous oxide (N_2O), trap heat from the sun and keep the planet warm enough to support life. However, human activities have exacerbated this effect by significantly increasing the concentration of these greenhouse gases in the atmosphere, leading to a warming planet. Fossil fuel burning for energy, transportation, and industry is the largest source of CO_2 emissions, while methane is primarily released from livestock, agriculture, and fossil fuel extraction (e.g., fracking).

The result is a feedback loop: as temperatures rise, it causes changes in the atmosphere, oceans, and land that accelerate further warming. For example, melting ice caps and glaciers reduce the Earth's ability to reflect sunlight (known as the albedo effect), causing more heat to be absorbed. Similarly, the thawing of permafrost in the Arctic releases vast quantities of stored methane, a potent greenhouse gas. These self-reinforcing processes risk pushing the climate system past critical tipping points, after which the warming could accelerate beyond our control.

Extreme Weather Events and Their Consequences

As the planet warms, we are seeing a marked increase in the frequency and severity of extreme weather events. These events are not just anomalies; they are the new normal, and they are already causing devastating impacts on people, ecosystems, and economies worldwide.

1. **Heatwaves**: More frequent and longer-lasting heatwaves are becoming a norm. In 2021, the Pacific Northwest of North America experienced record-breaking heat, with temperatures reaching 49.6°C (121.3°F) in Canada. Heatwaves like these strain power grids, trigger wildfires, exacerbate droughts, and cause an alarming rise in heat-related illnesses and deaths, particularly among vulnerable populations like the elderly and those with pre-existing health conditions.

2. **Wildfires**: Higher temperatures, combined with prolonged periods of drought, create the perfect conditions for wildfires to ignite and spread uncontrollably. The 2019-2020 Australian bushfires were some of the worst in recorded history, burning over 46 million acres, killing 3 billion animals, and releasing vast quantities of CO_2 into the atmosphere. The 2020 California wildfires burned more than 4 million acres, and the frequency of these fires in regions like the U.S. West, the Mediterranean, and Australia is expected to rise dramatically as temperatures continue to climb. Wildfires not only destroy ecosystems and property but also release stored carbon from vegetation and soil, further amplifying global warming.

3. **Hurricanes and Cyclones**: Warmer ocean temperatures increase the intensity of tropical storms, leading to stronger hurricanes and cyclones. The 2017 Atlantic hurricane season, which included Hurricane Harvey, Irma, and Maria, caused over $200 billion in damage and resulted in thousands of deaths. These storms are also intensifying in the Indian Ocean and South Pacific, causing widespread destruction and displacement. The increased rainfall and higher sea levels associated with climate change further exacerbate the damage from these storms, as we saw with Hurricane Katrina in 2005 and Super Typhoon Haiyan in 2013.

4. **Flooding and Sea Level Rise**: Rising sea levels, driven by glacial melting and the thermal expansion of seawater, pose a long-term threat to coastal cities and low-lying nations. In cities like Miami, New York, and Bangkok, the increased frequency of flooding due to rising tides and storm surges is already a daily challenge. Storm surge flooding is also becoming more severe, as higher sea levels make it easier for powerful hurricanes to flood coastlines. Coastal ecosystems like mangroves and wetlands that once acted as natural buffers against

flooding are disappearing due to human development and climate-induced damage, further intensifying the problem.

The Ripple Effect on Global Ecosystems and Human Health

While these extreme weather events have immediate and visible effects, the long-term consequences of climate change will be far-reaching and potentially irreversible. The interconnectedness of Earth's systems means that changes in one area can set off a chain reaction that affects everything from food production to human health.

- **Food Security**: Agriculture is particularly vulnerable to climate change. Rising temperatures and shifting rainfall patterns reduce crop yields, especially for staple crops like wheat, corn, and rice. As droughts and extreme weather events increase, water availability for irrigation will decrease, making it harder to sustain food production in many regions. In sub-Saharan Africa, for instance, crop production has already been severely impacted by climate-induced droughts, resulting in food shortages and rising prices. Global food security is at risk, with climate change exacerbating hunger and malnutrition for millions of people worldwide.

- **Health Impacts**: Climate change poses a significant threat to human health in multiple ways. The direct effects of extreme heat—heatstroke, dehydration, and heat-related illnesses—are already responsible for tens of thousands of deaths annually, particularly among vulnerable groups like the elderly and those without access to air conditioning. Vector-borne diseases such as malaria, dengue fever, and Lyme disease are expanding into new regions as warmer temperatures enable the spread of mosquitoes and ticks into areas that were previously too cold for them. Air pollution, which worsens with rising temperatures, is linked to respiratory diseases like asthma and chronic obstructive pulmonary disease (COPD), causing millions of premature deaths each year.

The science is clear: climate change is real, and its consequences are unfolding faster than we imagined. The window to limit global warming to 1.5°C—a target set by the Paris Agreement—is rapidly closing. If we are to avoid the worst effects of climate change—devastating sea-level rise, widespread food insecurity, extreme weather events, and ecosystem collapse—we must act with unprecedented urgency.

This means not only reducing carbon emissions but also investing in climate adaptation strategies to help communities prepare for the inevitable changes we will face. Renewable energy sources like solar, wind, and geothermal must replace fossil fuels, and we must work to protect and restore ecosystems that act as carbon sinks, such as forests, wetlands, and mangroves. These steps will require global cooperation, innovation, and bold leadership from all sectors of society—governments, corporations, communities, and individuals.

The path to a sustainable future depends on our willingness to confront the climate crisis head-on. The future of the planet and its inhabitants hinges on the decisions we make today. We must act now, or face the consequences of an increasingly unstable and inhospitable world.

Biodiversity Loss: The Sixth Mass Extinction

Biodiversity, the variety of life on Earth, forms the foundation of healthy ecosystems and plays an essential role in supporting life itself. From the smallest microbes in the soil to the largest apex predators in the ocean, every species, no matter how seemingly insignificant, is interconnected within a vast web of life that sustains the planet's ecological balance. Biodiversity is not just about the number of species; it's about the diversity of ecosystems, genetic variation, and the intricate relationships between organisms. These systems provide invaluable services such as pollination, carbon sequestration, water purification, and soil fertility—services that humanity depends on for survival.

However, we are currently facing the most rapid loss of biodiversity in the history of modern civilization. This crisis, often referred to as the Sixth Mass Extinction, is being driven by human activities, particularly habitat destruction, climate change, overexploitation of resources, and the introduction of invasive species. What is alarming is not just the scale of species loss but the fact that this is the first mass extinction event to be driven by human behavior. Unlike the previous five mass extinctions, which were caused by natural events such as volcanic eruptions or asteroid impacts, this sixth extinction is entirely within our power to prevent, or at least slow down.

The Rate of Extinction: A Grim Reality

In the past, Earth has witnessed five mass extinctions—events where more than 75% of species disappeared over relatively short periods. The most famous of these is the Cretaceous-Paleogene extinction event, which wiped out the dinosaurs around 66 million years ago. However, today, the rate of extinction is happening 100 to 1,000 times faster than the natural rate of extinction, with species disappearing at an unprecedented pace. According to the Intergovernmental Science-Policy Platform on Biodiversity and Ecosystem Services (IPBES), 1 million species are at risk of extinction within the next few decades. This includes not only iconic species like the tiger and the polar bear, but also lesser-known organisms, such as certain species of frogs, insects, and plants, which are essential for maintaining the health of ecosystems.

One of the starkest indicators of the biodiversity crisis is the collapse of insect populations, which are experiencing a global decline. Studies suggest that one-third of insect species are threatened with extinction, and some regions, like Europe, have already seen dramatic drops in insect populations, with declines of 75% or more in some areas. Insects, such as bees, butterflies, and moths, play a crucial role in pollination, which is vital for the reproduction of many of the plants we rely on for food. Their decline threatens the entire food web, as pollinators are responsible for the fertilization of 70% of flowering plants and about 35% of global food crops.

The loss of biodiversity also has cascading effects on ecosystems. When species go extinct, their roles in ecosystems—whether as predators, prey, decomposers, or pollinators—are left vacant, destabilizing the entire system. For example, the decline of apex predators such as wolves or sharks can lead to an overabundance of herbivores or smaller predators, which in turn disrupts the vegetation and prey species on which the ecosystem depends. This imbalance can have devastating consequences for both human and wildlife populations.

The Drivers of Biodiversity Loss

The causes of biodiversity loss are manifold, but they can largely be attributed to four main drivers, all of which are largely anthropogenic (human-caused):

1. **Habitat Destruction and Fragmentation**: The single greatest threat to biodiversity is the destruction of habitats through deforestation, urbanization, agriculture, and infrastructure development. The Amazon rainforest, often referred to as the "lungs of the Earth," is being cleared at an alarming rate to make way for cattle ranching, palm oil plantations, and logging. Tropical rainforests alone are home to more than 50% of the world's species, yet they are disappearing at a rate of around 10 million hectares (just under 25 million acres) per year. As habitats are destroyed or fragmented, species are often unable to find new homes or adapt to changing conditions. Deforestation in the Amazon not only threatens wildlife but also disrupts the global carbon cycle, contributing to climate change, which further exacerbates biodiversity loss.

2. **Climate Change**: Climate change is rapidly altering the natural environment in ways that species are ill-equipped to handle. Rising temperatures, changing precipitation patterns, and the increased frequency of extreme weather events like storms and droughts are pushing species beyond their tolerance limits. Many species, particularly those that live in specific habitats, such as polar bears in the Arctic or coral reefs in tropical oceans, are facing habitat loss or species migration as they cannot adapt to the changing climate fast enough. Furthermore, the altered timing of seasonal events like flowering, migration, and breeding is disrupting the synchrony of ecosystems, leading to cascading impacts throughout the food web.

3. **Overexploitation**: Overhunting, overfishing, and the illegal wildlife trade are major contributors to species loss. Commercial fishing has led to the collapse of fish populations worldwide, with species like the Atlantic cod nearly driven to extinction. In many regions, overhunting has decimated populations of large mammals, including elephants for their ivory, rhinos for their horns, and tigers for their pelts. The illegal wildlife trade is also responsible for the disappearance of countless other species, and it is worth noting that the black market for endangered species is valued at over $20 billion annually. Many of these species are also

important for maintaining ecosystem balance; for example, the removal of keystone species can unravel an entire ecosystem, as seen with the overhunting of wolves in Yellowstone National Park, which disrupted the park's ecosystem.

4. **Invasive Species**: The introduction of non-native species to ecosystems, whether intentionally or accidentally, is another driver of biodiversity loss. These invasive species often outcompete or prey on native species, causing them to decline or go extinct. For instance, the introduction of rats to islands has led to the extinction of numerous native bird species, and the spread of invasive plant species such as kudzu in the southeastern U.S. has choked out native vegetation. The problem of invasive species is particularly acute in areas like islands or isolated ecosystems, where native species have evolved without the presence of such predators or competitors.

The Impact of Biodiversity Loss on Ecosystem Services

The loss of biodiversity goes beyond the extinction of charismatic species; it threatens the very ecosystem services that humanity depends on for survival. Ecosystem services are the processes through which nature provides us with vital resources—clean water, fertile soil, climate regulation, and the regulation of disease. These services are the foundation of our economy, health, and well-being.

1. **Pollination**: As we discussed earlier, many of the world's food crops depend on pollinators like bees, butterflies, and birds. The decline of these species poses a direct threat to global food security, with some studies estimating that around 35% of global food crops rely on animal pollination. Without these vital creatures, food production would be severely compromised, leading to price increases and food shortages.

2. **Soil Health and Agriculture**: Soil biodiversity, which includes a variety of microorganisms, fungi, and insects, is essential for maintaining healthy soil, which in turn supports agricultural productivity. The loss of soil biodiversity can lead to soil degradation, reduced crop yields, and increased vulnerability to erosion and desertification. This is a direct threat to food security and agricultural livelihoods, particularly in regions that are already vulnerable to climate change.

3. **Carbon Sequestration and Climate Regulation**: Forests, wetlands, and oceans play a critical role in regulating the global climate by acting as carbon sinks— absorbing carbon dioxide (CO_2) from the atmosphere and mitigating the effects of climate change. The destruction of forests or the degradation of wetlands reduces the planet's capacity to sequester carbon, further accelerating global warming. For instance, tropical forests store approximately one-third of the world's carbon in their biomass. If these forests are destroyed or degraded, this stored carbon is released into the atmosphere, exacerbating the climate crisis.

4.   **Water Purification**: Wetlands, forests, and healthy river systems act as natural filters for water, purifying it of toxins, sediment, and pathogens. The destruction of these ecosystems can lead to increased pollution in rivers and lakes, endangering drinking water supplies and leading to waterborne diseases.

5.   **Medicinal Resources**: Many of the medicines we use today are derived from plants, animals, and microorganisms. The loss of biodiversity reduces the pool of potential compounds for new pharmaceutical discoveries, limiting our ability to treat diseases and improve health outcomes. Traditional medicine—which relies heavily on local biodiversity—is also at risk as species disappear from their native habitats.

Can We Stop the Sixth Mass Extinction?

The future is not entirely hopeless. While the situation is dire, there is still time to slow down the pace of extinction and preserve the biodiversity that remains. By implementing large-scale conservation efforts, halting deforestation, expanding protected areas, and reducing our carbon footprint, we can make a significant impact. Restoring habitats, particularly mangroves, wetlands, and coral reefs, can also help bolster ecosystems and reduce the impact of climate change.

Moreover, we must address the root causes of biodiversity loss: unsustainable development, overconsumption, and inequity. Conservation efforts must be linked with sustainable practices in agriculture, forestry, fisheries, and urban planning to ensure a future where both people and nature can thrive.

The loss of biodiversity is not just an environmental issue—it is a human issue. Our survival depends on the health of ecosystems, and the loss of species and habitats will only make it more difficult to meet our needs in the future. The Sixth Mass Extinction is a clarion call for urgent action.

Pollution: The Contamination of Our World

Pollution is perhaps the most pervasive and insidious environmental problem of our time. It's everywhere. It enters our air, water, and soil, affecting every aspect of the natural world and human life. Unlike other environmental crises, pollution often operates silently, its impacts accumulating over time, often invisible to the naked eye. However, the consequences are profound: polluting activities directly harm ecosystems, human health, and even the global economy. Pollution is not just a localized issue; it is a global threat, affecting every country, community, and individual, regardless of borders.

Pollution is driven by industrialization, urbanization, agricultural practices, and the relentless demand for consumer goods. It is a byproduct of the way we produce, consume, and dispose of products, and it has created a legacy of contamination that will last for generations. From toxic air to polluted rivers, oceans filled with plastic, and soil contaminated by pesticides and heavy metals, pollution has become an inseparable part of modern life.

Air Pollution: Breathing in the Poison

One of the most visible and dangerous forms of pollution is air pollution, which directly impacts human health and the climate. Every year, 7 million people globally die prematurely due to airborne pollutants—this includes particulate matter (PM2.5), ozone, nitrogen dioxide, and sulfur dioxide, among others. Air pollution is primarily caused by the burning of fossil fuels, including coal, oil, and natural gas, which are used in transportation, energy production, and industry. Agricultural practices, such as livestock farming and the use of synthetic fertilizers, also contribute significantly to air pollution by releasing methane and ammonia into the atmosphere.

The worst air quality tends to be concentrated in urban areas, where vehicle emissions, industrial processes, and construction activities create a toxic soup of pollutants. Cities like Delhi, Beijing, and Mexico City frequently exceed the **World Health Organization's (WHO)** air quality standards. In these regions, residents are regularly exposed to levels of air pollution that are more than 10 times the safe limits. The long-term effects of breathing in polluted air are severe: respiratory diseases, cardiovascular diseases, and lung cancer are rampant in areas with chronic air pollution. Furthermore, children, the elderly, and low-income communities are disproportionately affected, as they often live in areas with the poorest air quality.

Even more insidious is the impact of air pollution on the climate. Many air pollutants, such as black carbon (soot), methane, and tropospheric ozone, are also greenhouse gases, meaning they contribute to global warming. For example, black carbon absorbs sunlight and heats the atmosphere, making it a significant driver of climate change, particularly in polar regions where it accelerates the melting of glaciers and ice caps.

Water Pollution: Contaminating Our Lifeblood

Water is essential to life, but it is under constant assault from pollutants that degrade its quality and, ultimately, its ability to support ecosystems and human societies. Water pollution can be caused by a variety of factors, from industrial discharge, agricultural runoff, plastic waste, and untreated sewage, to the use of toxic chemicals in urban and rural areas.

1. **Industrial and Agricultural Runoff**: The most common pollutants in water bodies are chemicals from industries and agriculture. The agriculture sector is responsible for around 70% of water usage globally, and runoff from fertilizers and pesticides has a devastating impact on water quality. These chemicals contaminate rivers, lakes, and groundwater supplies, making them unsuitable for drinking and agricultural use. Nitrates, found in fertilizers, can lead to eutrophication, a process where water bodies become overloaded with nutrients,

leading to the growth of toxic algae blooms. These blooms reduce oxygen levels in water, killing fish and other aquatic life, and in some cases, can produce toxic substances that harm wildlife and humans. For example, the Flint water crisis in Michigan exposed how toxic substances like lead in water can have devastating effects on human health, particularly in children, leading to lifelong developmental issues.

2. **Plastic Pollution**: One of the most visible forms of water pollution is plastic pollution, which has reached catastrophic levels. Approximately 8 million metric tons of plastic waste enter the oceans every year, and it is estimated that there will be more plastic in the oceans than fish by 2050 if current trends continue. This plastic waste, ranging from microplastics to discarded fishing nets, threatens marine life, from sea turtles that mistake plastic bags for jellyfish to whales that ingest massive amounts of plastic debris, leading to injury and death. Plastic also leaches toxic chemicals into the water, which accumulate in the food chain, eventually reaching humans through seafood consumption. These pollutants also disrupt the reproductive systems of marine species, leading to population declines and biodiversity loss.

3. **Chemical Contaminants**: In addition to the obvious pollutants, there are invisible chemicals that contaminate water supplies, with devastating effects. Heavy metals like mercury, lead, and arsenic, used in mining, manufacturing, and agriculture, find their way into waterways and pose serious health risks. Ingesting or coming into contact with these chemicals can cause severe neurological disorders, cancer, and kidney damage. Pesticides like DDT and newer chemicals like neonicotinoids persist in the environment, poisoning aquatic life and polluting drinking water. These chemicals, often used to control pests or improve crop yields, have long-lasting impacts on both ecosystems and human health.

Soil Pollution: The Silent Crisis Beneath Our Feet

Soil pollution is one of the most underappreciated yet pervasive forms of contamination, with significant consequences for food production, water quality, and overall ecosystem health. Soil pollution occurs when harmful chemicals, including heavy metals, pesticides, and industrial waste, are deposited into the ground, making the soil toxic and unable to support healthy plant life.

1. **Pesticide and Fertilizer Use**: Intensive agricultural practices often rely on the widespread use of synthetic fertilizers and pesticides, which contribute to soil contamination. Over time, these chemicals degrade soil quality, kill beneficial microorganisms, and leach into groundwater, further polluting drinking water sources. Pesticides, particularly organophosphates, are linked to a wide range of environmental problems, including bee colony collapse, which threatens pollination and food production. They also pose direct health risks to agricultural workers and communities living near farms.

2. **Industrial Waste and Heavy Metals**: Industrial waste, including toxic chemicals and heavy metals like cadmium, lead, and arsenic, is often dumped into the soil without proper treatment. These contaminants accumulate over time, making the soil unsuitable for growing crops and causing long-term health hazards for humans who consume the contaminated produce. A particularly troubling example is the contamination of farmland with lead from the use of leaded gasoline and batteries. Heavy metals in soil also enter the food chain through bioaccumulation, causing chronic health problems in humans and animals that ingest contaminated plants and animals.

3. **Waste Disposal**: Improper disposal of waste, especially e-waste (discarded electronics), contributes to soil pollution. As electronics such as smartphones, computers, and batteries degrade in landfills, they release toxic substances like lead, cadmium, and mercury into the soil, creating hotspots of contamination. These pollutants can leach into water supplies, affecting both plant and animal life. The global rise in e-waste is creating a growing crisis, as discarded electronics are often improperly handled, particularly in developing countries.

The Global Health Impacts of Pollution

Pollution doesn't just harm the environment—it's a direct threat to human health. The World Health Organization (WHO) estimates that 9 million people die prematurely every year due to exposure to environmental pollution. Pollution is responsible for diseases ranging from respiratory illnesses like asthma and chronic obstructive pulmonary disease (COPD) to cancers, neurological disorders, and cardiovascular diseases.

In particular, children and low-income communities are disproportionately affected by pollution. Children's developing bodies are more vulnerable to pollutants, and they often live in neighborhoods with higher levels of pollution. Air pollution, for example, has been linked to impaired lung development in children, increased rates of asthma, and even reduced cognitive function. The impact of pollution on vulnerable populations, including indigenous communities near mining sites or toxic waste dumps, is an urgent humanitarian issue.

Addressing Pollution: From Prevention to Cleanup

Tackling the global pollution crisis requires a multifaceted approach. We must reduce pollution at its source through stricter regulations, cleaner production technologies, and sustainable consumption practices. This includes transitioning away from fossil fuels to renewable energy, banning or restricting harmful chemicals, and implementing zero-waste policies. Furthermore, we must invest in innovative solutions to clean up existing pollution. Technologies such as bioremediation, which uses microorganisms to break down pollutants, and clean-up programs for plastic waste, are part of the solution.

Ultimately, the fight against pollution is one of prevention and restoration. By changing the way we produce, consume, and dispose of goods, we can create a healthier world for future generations. However, this will require global cooperation, the support of businesses to adopt sustainable practices, and the commitment of governments to enact and enforce strong environmental regulations. It's time to tackle pollution with the urgency it demands, before it irreversibly alters the planet's ecosystems and threatens the future of humanity itself.

Water Scarcity: A Looming Crisis

Water is the most fundamental resource on Earth. It sustains life, shapes ecosystems, and drives economies. From quenching thirst and irrigating crops to generating electricity and supporting industries, water is essential for nearly every aspect of human life. Yet, despite its critical importance, we are facing a global water crisis that threatens to disrupt every facet of civilization. Water scarcity—the lack of sufficient fresh water to meet the needs of a population—is becoming one of the most pressing environmental challenges of the 21st century.

By 2050, it is projected that nearly two-thirds of the world's population could experience water scarcity, with 1.8 billion people living in areas with absolute water scarcity. The crisis is already unfolding in many parts of the world, from the Middle East and North Africa to parts of Asia, South America, and sub-Saharan Africa. As populations grow, climate change exacerbates existing water shortages, and our continued misuse of water resources accelerates the crisis. The consequences of this crisis are far-reaching—affecting everything from human health to agriculture, biodiversity, and geopolitics.

Understanding Water Scarcity: The Types and Causes

Water scarcity can be broadly classified into two categories: physical scarcity and economic scarcity.

1. **Physical Scarcity** occurs when natural freshwater resources are insufficient to meet the demands of a region's population. This typically happens in areas where there is limited freshwater supply due to geographic location or climatic conditions—such as arid or semi-arid regions. Desert regions like the Middle East and North Africa are prime examples, where water resources are scarce, and demand far exceeds the available supply.

2. **Economic Scarcity**, on the other hand, arises not from a lack of water resources but from poor infrastructure, inefficient management, or political instability. Even in countries with abundant water resources, such as parts of Asia or Africa, poor governance and inequitable distribution can prevent access to water. In these regions, the issue is often not the availability of water, but the lack of access due to poverty, poor water management, or conflict. For example, while India has a relatively high per capita water availability, rapid urbanization, increased water

demand from agriculture, and poor water infrastructure have led to widespread water shortages in many areas.

The Global Scale of Water Scarcity

Water scarcity is a global phenomenon that affects countries at different levels, but it disproportionately impacts vulnerable regions. Around the world, 2 billion people already live in areas experiencing high water stress, meaning that water use exceeds 40% of available resources. The situation is likely to worsen due to several key factors:

1. **Population Growth and Urbanization**: By 2050, the world's population is expected to reach nearly 10 billion, with much of this growth occurring in regions that already face water shortages. As urban populations expand, so does the demand for clean water for drinking, sanitation, and industrial use. The concentration of large populations in cities exacerbates competition for water and strains existing infrastructure.

2. **Agricultural Demand**: Agriculture accounts for approximately 70% of global water use. Irrigation—used to grow the food that feeds the world—places an immense strain on freshwater resources, particularly in water-scarce regions. Crops such as rice, wheat, and cotton require vast amounts of water to grow, and water-intensive livestock farming compounds this issue. As global food demand rises, this stress will only increase. The over-extraction of water for agricultural purposes in areas like India and the U.S. West has led to the depletion of aquifers and the drying up of rivers.

3. **Climate Change**: Perhaps the most insidious threat to global water availability is climate change. As temperatures rise, droughts become more severe, and precipitation patterns become more unpredictable. Areas that are already arid will experience even greater water shortages, while others may face flooding as intense storms overwhelm local water management systems. Climate change is also affecting the timing and quantity of snowmelt in mountainous regions, which serves as a key water source for millions of people. The Himalayas, Andes, and Rocky Mountains provide seasonal water to regions where snowmelt feeds rivers, but with rising temperatures, these glaciers are retreating at alarming rates, threatening the availability of water during dry months.

4. **Pollution and Contamination**: The contamination of water resources with industrial waste, agricultural runoff, plastic debris, and sewage has further compounded the scarcity problem. Polluted water supplies are not just unusable—they are dangerous. In regions where freshwater sources are already limited, contamination makes clean water more difficult to access and forces millions of people to rely on unsafe sources. In countries like India, China, and parts of sub-Saharan Africa, high levels of water pollution have made freshwater undrinkable, further stressing already scarce resources.

The Effects of Water Scarcity: A Multidimensional Crisis

Water scarcity affects every facet of human life, from health to agriculture, economic stability, and geopolitical relations. Let's take a closer look at how the crisis manifests:

1. **Human Health**: Lack of access to clean water is directly linked to a wide range of health problems, including waterborne diseases such as cholera, dysentery, and typhoid fever. According to the World Health Organization (WHO), approximately 2.1 billion people lack access to safe drinking water, and an estimated 500,000 deaths annually are attributed to diarrhea alone. Lack of water also hampers sanitation and hygiene, contributing to the spread of infectious diseases. Poor access to water disproportionately impacts children, particularly in developing countries, where poor sanitation systems and contaminated water sources are widespread.

2. **Agricultural Crisis and Food Security**: Water scarcity is inextricably linked to the global food crisis. Without adequate water, crops cannot thrive, and livestock cannot be adequately sustained. This leads to food insecurity, increased food prices, and displaced farmers. In areas already prone to droughts, such as parts of Africa and the Middle East, water shortages exacerbate hunger and malnutrition. The impact of water scarcity on agriculture is particularly concerning given that global food production will need to increase by 70% to feed the growing population. Without access to water for irrigation, it is unlikely that this target will be met, leading to global food shortages and escalating poverty.

3. **Economic Instability**: Water scarcity is an economic issue as much as it is an environmental one. Many industries, including textile production, mining, energy generation, and food processing, require large amounts of water. In regions with high water stress, industries must either reduce production or face higher operational costs due to limited water supply. Agriculture, which employs millions worldwide, suffers significantly when crops fail because of insufficient water. As water prices increase, access becomes even more inequitable, further deepening social inequality and poverty.

4. **Geopolitical Tensions**: As freshwater becomes scarcer, competition for access to water resources is growing, leading to potential conflict. Many of the world's largest rivers—such as the Nile, Jordan, Indus, and Ganges—flow through multiple countries, each with different water demands and competing interests. Disputes over shared rivers have already led to political tensions and military confrontations, particularly in regions where water resources are vital for agriculture and industry. As countries experience greater water stress, it is possible that water wars—conflicts driven by access to freshwater—could become more frequent.

5.   **Ecosystem Collapse**: Water scarcity also leads to the degradation of natural ecosystems. Freshwater ecosystems, such as rivers, lakes, wetlands, and aquifers, provide vital habitats for countless species of plants and animals. When these water sources dry up, aquatic ecosystems collapse, leading to the loss of biodiversity. Wetlands, which act as natural filters and carbon sinks, are particularly vulnerable to drought and water extraction. The depletion of rivers and groundwater also disrupts agricultural land and wildlife habitats, making it more difficult for species to survive.

Solutions to Water Scarcity: What Can Be Done?

Addressing water scarcity requires a holistic approach that includes conservation, efficient water management, policy reforms, and technological innovations. Several key strategies can help alleviate the crisis:

1.   **Water Conservation**: Efforts to reduce water consumption are critical in mitigating the impact of water scarcity. Governments and industries can promote water-saving technologies, encourage water-efficient agricultural practices, and improve water infrastructure to reduce waste.

2.   **Desalination**: Desalination—the process of removing salt from seawater—has the potential to significantly increase freshwater availability in water-scarce regions. While desalination technology is expensive and energy-intensive, advances in renewable energy and efficient desalination technologies can help make it more accessible.

3.   **Rainwater Harvesting**: Collecting and storing rainwater can help provide a reliable source of freshwater in areas with unpredictable rainfall patterns. This technology is already being employed in many parts of the world, including India, Australia, and the Middle East.

4.   **Recycling and Reusing Water**: Implementing water recycling and reuse systems, particularly in industries and cities, can help extend the lifespan of available water resources. Greywater recycling, where water from baths, sinks, and washing machines is reused for irrigation or industrial purposes, can reduce demand on freshwater sources.

5.   **Policy Reforms and International Cooperation**: Stronger governance and water management policies are essential. Countries must establish water rights agreements for shared resources and ensure equitable distribution of water. International bodies like the United Nations can play a crucial role in facilitating cooperation over transboundary water resources, ensuring that peaceful solutions are found in water-scarce regions.

Water scarcity is a crisis we cannot ignore. We must take immediate action to protect and manage this precious resource to ensure a sustainable and equitable future for all.

As we look at these environmental challenges—climate change, biodiversity loss, pollution, and water scarcity—it becomes evident that they are not isolated problems. They are deeply interconnected, each issue feeding into the other in a complex web of cause and effect. The devastation of one ecosystem leads to the collapse of another, and the degradation of our environment makes it harder to adapt to the changes we are already experiencing. If we are to address these issues effectively, we must do so with an understanding of their interconnectedness and a sense of urgency.

The Interconnectedness of These Crises

When we talk about the environmental challenges facing the world today—climate change, biodiversity loss, pollution, water scarcity, and so on—it's essential to understand that these crises do not exist in isolation. They are deeply interconnected, each one influencing and exacerbating the others in a complex web of cause and effect. Our actions in one area of environmental concern often trigger cascading impacts in others, making it even more urgent to adopt integrated, holistic solutions.

In fact, the systems that sustain life on Earth—climate, ecosystems, water cycles, and human society—are all tightly interconnected. Disrupting one aspect of this balance often causes ripples that affect everything from food security to global health. A disruption of the water cycle, for example, doesn't just result in drought or flooding—it can lead to crop failure, food insecurity, and the collapse of local economies. Similarly, pollution doesn't only harm the environment; it directly contributes to climate change, damages human health, and accelerates the degradation of vital natural systems like soil fertility and biodiversity.

By examining the intersections between the most pressing global crises, we can gain a clearer understanding of the stakes involved and the importance of a coordinated response.

Climate Change and Biodiversity Loss: A Vicious Cycle

The most glaring example of interconnectedness is the relationship between climate change and biodiversity loss. Climate change, driven by human activities such as the burning of fossil fuels and deforestation, is the single largest driver of species extinction today. Rising temperatures, shifting weather patterns, and more frequent extreme weather events are disrupting ecosystems, leading to habitat loss and species displacement. Animals that once thrived in stable, predictable climates are finding it difficult to adapt to rapid changes in temperature, precipitation, and food availability.

One example is the polar bear, whose habitat in the Arctic is rapidly disappearing as the sea ice melts due to warming temperatures. Not only are polar bears directly threatened by loss of habitat, but the melting ice also disrupts the marine food chain, affecting everything from krill to fish populations that the bears rely on for food. Similarly, coral reefs, which host a staggering array of marine life, are particularly vulnerable to rising ocean temperatures and ocean acidification—both driven by climate change. As reefs bleach and die off, entire marine ecosystems are collapsing, leaving countless species without food or shelter.

On the other hand, the loss of biodiversity further exacerbates climate change. Healthy ecosystems, such as forests and wetlands, act as carbon sinks, absorbing large amounts of carbon dioxide from the atmosphere. When species go extinct and ecosystems are destroyed, these natural carbon buffers are lost. For instance, tropical rainforests like the Amazon store massive amounts of carbon. As these forests are cleared for agriculture or urban development, the carbon stored in the trees is released back into the atmosphere, worsening global warming. Additionally, the loss of plant species reduces the ability of ecosystems to sequester carbon, creating a feedback loop that accelerates both climate change and biodiversity loss.

Pollution and Climate Change: The Double Threat

Another key intersection is the relationship between pollution and climate change. Much of the pollution we generate, particularly from the burning of fossil fuels, directly contributes to global warming. Carbon dioxide (CO_2), methane (CH_4), and other greenhouse gases are released into the atmosphere through industrial processes, agriculture, and transportation, trapping heat and causing the planet to warm. However, pollution doesn't just worsen the climate—it also accelerates environmental degradation, contributing to a range of additional problems.

For example, air pollution from burning coal, oil, and natural gas releases fine particulate matter (PM2.5) that harms human health, but these same emissions also contribute to the buildup of greenhouse gases. Black carbon (soot) is another pollutant with a dual impact: it not only affects air quality but also contributes to global warming by absorbing sunlight and warming the atmosphere. The combination of health problems caused by air pollution and the worsening climate crisis makes this a particularly dangerous area of concern. The more polluted the air becomes, the more difficult it is to slow climate change and protect vulnerable populations.

Plastic pollution provides another example of the interconnection between pollution and climate change. Over 8 million tons of plastic enter the oceans each year, affecting marine life and ecosystems. However, plastic production itself is highly carbon-intensive. The manufacturing of plastic is a major contributor to fossil fuel consumption, while plastic waste that ends up in landfills or the ocean emits methane as it decomposes. Furthermore, the fossil fuel industry is not just a major source of pollution—its reliance on petroleum products like plastic is directly linked to the increase in greenhouse gases.

Water Scarcity and Climate Change: A Dangerous Partnership

Water scarcity is another critical issue that is tightly linked to both climate change and pollution. Climate change is altering precipitation patterns, leading to both droughts in some areas and floods in others. For example, California and Australia are experiencing more intense and prolonged droughts, leading to water shortages, crop failures, and wildfires. In contrast, regions like Bangladesh and parts of India are witnessing more frequent and devastating floods due to the increased frequency of extreme weather events, including monsoon rains and cyclones.

As temperatures rise, glaciers and snowpacks—which many regions rely on for freshwater supplies—are melting at unprecedented rates. This is especially critical for populations in mountainous regions such as the Himalayas, the Andes, and the Rocky Mountains, where glacial meltwater provides a significant portion of freshwater throughout the year. The loss of glaciers and the alteration of seasonal snowmelt will leave millions of people without reliable access to clean water.

Moreover, pollution contributes to water scarcity. Agricultural runoff, which contains harmful pesticides, fertilizers, and animal waste, is a major contaminant of freshwater supplies. The excess nutrients from fertilizers lead to eutrophication, where water bodies become overloaded with nutrients, creating dead zones where no life can survive. Wastewater from industrial and municipal sources also contributes to water pollution, further diminishing the availability of clean water for drinking, agriculture, and sanitation.

The Link Between Poverty, Water Scarcity, and Health

Water scarcity is not only an environmental issue—it's a social justice issue. Access to clean water is essential for health, education, and economic prosperity. In many parts of the world, particularly in sub-Saharan Africa and parts of Asia, people are already suffering from the combined effects of water scarcity, inadequate sanitation, and pollution. In India, for instance, millions of people still lack access to clean drinking water, and women and children often spend hours each day collecting water from distant and contaminated sources. The lack of access to clean water exacerbates poverty, malnutrition, and disease, and it makes it difficult for children to attend school or for communities to develop economically.

The intersection of poverty, water scarcity, and pollution creates a vicious cycle. As communities grow poorer due to a lack of clean water, they are less able to invest in infrastructure or adopt water-efficient technologies. This leaves them more vulnerable to climate change and pollution, while simultaneously reducing their capacity to recover from disasters like floods or droughts. This cycle disproportionately affects the global South, where both the effects of climate change and the legacy of colonial exploitation have left communities especially vulnerable.

Solutions Require Integrated Thinking

The reality of these interconnected crises underscores the need for integrated solutions—approaches that recognize the complex ways in which climate change, biodiversity loss, pollution, water scarcity, and social inequity are intertwined. A successful response to these challenges will require not only addressing individual issues but also understanding how they reinforce one another and contribute to global instability.

1. **Climate and Water Solutions**: Sustainable water management must be integrated into climate adaptation strategies. This includes rainwater harvesting, water-efficient agricultural practices, and the restoration of ecosystems like wetlands and forests that naturally regulate water cycles.

2. **Pollution and Conservation**: Tackling pollution and promoting conservation must go hand in hand. Protecting and restoring ecosystems, particularly those that are carbon-rich (like forests and wetlands), can help mitigate climate change, prevent water pollution, and preserve biodiversity.

3. **Inclusive and Just Solutions**: Solutions must also be equitable, ensuring that vulnerable populations, such as marginalized communities, women, and children, are included in the conversation. Addressing social inequalities in access to resources like water and clean air will be essential to building resilience and equity in the face of these crises.

In the face of these interconnected environmental crises, there is no silver bullet. No single policy or action will suffice. Instead, we must approach environmental issues with a systems-thinking mindset, recognizing the web of interconnections that bind them and understanding that real solutions lie in holistic, integrated strategies. The future of the planet—and the survival of humanity—depends on our ability to see these crises as parts of a whole and to act accordingly.

Real-Life Examples: How These Issues Are Affecting People, Ecosystems, and Economies Today

While the statistics, studies, and projections can paint a sobering picture of the environmental crises we face, it is in the real-life stories of individuals, communities, and ecosystems where the true impact of these challenges comes to life. From the Amazon rainforest to the Arctic Circle, the effects of climate change, biodiversity loss, pollution, and water scarcity are already being felt in profound and often devastating ways. These real-world examples not only illustrate the scale of the problems but also highlight the urgency of action.

1. The Amazon Rainforest: Deforestation, Climate Change, and Biodiversity Loss

The Amazon rainforest—often referred to as the "lungs of the planet"—is one of the most vital ecosystems in the world. It absorbs vast amounts of carbon dioxide, regulates the global climate, and supports one in ten species on Earth. However, the Amazon is under siege. Deforestation driven by illegal logging, agricultural expansion, and mining is rapidly reducing its size and health. Since 2000, over 10% of the Amazon rainforest has been destroyed, a trend that is accelerating under pressure from political and economic interests.

The consequences of Amazon deforestation go far beyond the loss of trees. First, as trees are cleared, they release carbon dioxide back into the atmosphere, contributing directly to global warming. Second, the destruction of this vast ecosystem disrupts biodiversity on an unimaginable scale. Species such as the jaguar, macaws, and poison dart frogs are losing their natural habitats, and many are on the brink of extinction. In fact, the Amazon is currently experiencing what experts call a "tipping point", where deforestation is creating feedback loops that make it harder for the forest to regenerate. Droughts, driven by climate change, exacerbate this cycle, and large parts of the forest could soon become a savannah, altering not just local ecosystems but global climate patterns.

The indigenous communities living in the Amazon are also feeling the effects of this environmental destruction. These groups rely on the forest for food, water, medicine, and cultural identity. As forests are cleared, they are being displaced from their lands, and their ways of life are being threatened. Despite their small population, Indigenous people play a critical role in the preservation of the forest, using traditional knowledge to sustainably manage the land. Yet, their voices are often ignored or suppressed, particularly in regions where illegal logging and mining are rampant.

2. The Arctic: Melting Ice, Rising Seas, and Indigenous Communities

The Arctic is warming at nearly three times the global average due to climate change, a phenomenon known as Arctic amplification. As temperatures rise, the ice sheets and glaciers that cover the region are melting at an alarming rate. The Arctic sea ice has shrunk by more than 40% over the last few decades, and the Greenland ice sheet is losing mass at an accelerating rate. This meltwater is contributing significantly to global sea-level rise, threatening coastal communities worldwide, from the Maldives to New York City.

But the impacts aren't just global—they are deeply felt in the Arctic itself. Indigenous communities such as the Inuit in Canada and Alaska are witnessing the destruction of their traditional way of life. For centuries, they have relied on ice fishing, whaling, and hunting as vital parts of their culture and livelihoods. However, the shrinking ice cover has made it increasingly difficult to access hunting grounds and travel by traditional means, such as dog sleds or snowmobiles. Permafrost—the permanently frozen ground that underpins much of the Arctic landscape—is also beginning to thaw, which causes ground to become unstable, leading to erosion, landslides, and the collapse of buildings and infrastructure.

As the ice melts, new shipping routes are opening up, leading to increased human activity in the region, including resource extraction and tourism. The region's unique ecosystems and fragile biodiversity are at risk, with species like the polar bear and the Arctic fox losing their habitats as the ice disappears. The melting of the Arctic sea ice also affects global climate systems by decreasing the Earth's albedo (its ability to reflect sunlight), accelerating the warming of the planet.

3. The Great Barrier Reef: Coral Bleaching and Ocean Acidification

The Great Barrier Reef in Australia, one of the most biodiverse ecosystems on the planet, is also in peril. Over the past few decades, the reef has experienced widespread coral bleaching events caused by rising sea temperatures. As the ocean warms, coral polyps expel the algae living inside them, causing the coral to lose its color and become more vulnerable to disease. The 2016 and 2017 bleaching events were among the most severe, and scientists warn that we are nearing the point where the reef may not recover from these stressors.

In addition to bleaching, the increased acidification of the oceans, driven by rising atmospheric CO2, is weakening the calcium carbonate skeletons that corals depend on for structure and protection. As a result, the coral reef is becoming more fragile and unable to withstand the growing pressures from both climate change and human activities like overfishing and pollution.

The destruction of the Great Barrier Reef has far-reaching consequences. The reef supports thousands of species of fish, mollusks, and other marine life, and is a major source of income for Australia's fishing and tourism industries. In 2018, the reef supported an estimated $6 billion Australian dollars in revenue from tourism alone. The collapse of the reef would not only devastate marine biodiversity but would also hurt the livelihoods of millions of people who depend on it for food, jobs, and cultural identity.

4. California: Drought, Wildfires, and Water Mismanagement

California, a state long known for its agricultural productivity, is facing some of the most severe environmental crises in the United States. Over the past two decades, droughts have become more frequent and severe due to climate change, reducing the water supply available for irrigation, drinking, and industrial use. The state is experiencing an increased frequency of wildfires, which are fueled by dry conditions, heatwaves, and human activity. In 2020 alone, over 4 million acres of land were scorched by wildfires, leading to the destruction of homes, businesses, and entire communities. The smoke from these fires blanketed vast areas of the country, contributing to poor air quality and increased respiratory illnesses.

Water scarcity is a major concern, particularly in agriculture-heavy regions like the Central Valley, where farmers depend on irrigation to grow crops. However, as water becomes more scarce, farmers are faced with the tough choice of whether to divert water for agricultural use or leave it for municipal and industrial needs. In many cases, over-extraction of water from critical sources like the Colorado River and Sacramento-San Joaquin River Delta has led to environmental degradation, affecting both the natural ecosystems and the livelihoods of those who rely on these waters.

California's water management system, designed in the early 20th century, has long been criticized for its inefficiency, waste, and inequitable distribution. Large agricultural operations often receive more water than the state's urban populations or ecosystems. Despite being one of the world's leading agricultural producers, California's water system is under increasing stress as the state grapples with its complex relationship between growing populations, agriculture, and climate change.

5. Cape Town, South Africa: Day Zero and the Threat of Water Shortages

In 2018, Cape Town, South Africa, came dangerously close to becoming the first major city in the world to run out of water. The phenomenon known as Day Zero was triggered by a combination of drought, climate change, and over-extraction of the city's water resources. Cape Town's primary water supply, the Theewaterskloof Dam, reached a crisis point after three consecutive years of low rainfall, and the city was forced to take extreme measures to conserve water.

During the Day Zero crisis, residents were faced with severe water rationing. Water supplies were limited to a few liters per person per day, and water distribution points were set up across the city for people to collect water. While the city managed to avert disaster through significant conservation efforts, the event highlighted the dangers of water mismanagement and the vulnerability of cities to the effects of climate change.

In the aftermath of Day Zero, Cape Town invested heavily in alternative water sources, such as desalination and recycled wastewater, and implemented strict water conservation policies. However, the crisis is far from over. As climate change continues to alter weather patterns, cities like Cape Town—and others around the world—will face growing pressure to adapt to water scarcity. This event serves as a stark reminder that water, once taken for granted in many urban areas, is becoming a precious and limited resource.

These real-life examples offer just a glimpse into the complex and often devastating impacts of the environmental crises we are facing. The Amazon rainforest, the Arctic, California, Cape Town, and the Great Barrier Reef are not isolated cases—they are reflections of a global trend that connects every corner of the world. The urgency of addressing these issues cannot be overstated. As we witness these crises unfold in real-time, we must take responsibility for the role we have played in exacerbating them—and, more importantly, we must recognize the opportunity we have to create change. These real-life stories show us that the time to act is now.

Chapter 2

Corporate Greed and the Obstruction of Progress

The scale and scope of the environmental crises we face today are undeniably vast, but one of the central forces driving these challenges is the immense power and influence wielded by large corporations. For decades, profit-driven motives have shaped corporate policies and practices in ways that often prioritize short-term financial gain over the long-term health of the planet. From fossil fuel giants to agribusinesses, chemical manufacturers, and even tech companies, these entities have played a central role in contributing to environmental degradation across the globe.

While some corporations have made attempts to greenwash their images or tout environmental initiatives, the reality is that many of the world's largest companies are still deeply embedded in activities that exploit natural resources, pollute ecosystems, and exacerbate climate change. This chapter will explore how corporate greed and the pursuit of profits often trump sustainable practices, resulting in significant harm to the environment. By examining specific industries and their impact, we can better understand the need for stronger regulations and consumer pressure to force meaningful change.

The Fossil Fuel Industry: The Engine of Climate Change

Perhaps no industry is as synonymous with environmental degradation as the fossil fuel sector. The extraction, refinement, and burning of oil, coal, and natural gas have been the primary drivers of global warming. The carbon dioxide (CO_2) emissions generated by these processes have been the single largest contributor to the greenhouse effect, which causes global temperatures to rise, disrupts ecosystems, and leads to extreme weather events. Yet, the fossil fuel industry continues to be one of the most powerful and profitable industries in the world, with massive companies like ExxonMobil, Chevron, Shell, and BP reaping billions of dollars in profits year after year, even as they wreak havoc on the environment.

In 2021, for example, the top five oil and gas companies—**ExxonMobil, Shell, BP, Chevron, and TotalEnergies**—collectively posted more than $51 billion in profits. While many companies have announced commitments to reducing carbon emissions or transitioning to renewable energy, their actual investments in clean energy are minimal compared to their investments in fossil fuel extraction. ExxonMobil, for instance, has faced criticism for spending more than $15 billion a year on oil and gas production while spending just a fraction on renewable energy alternatives.

Beyond emissions, fossil fuel companies are responsible for oil spills, deforestation, and land degradation through the extraction processes. Fracking—a method used to extract oil and natural gas from deep underground—has been linked to water contamination, earthquakes, and methane emissions. Additionally, the industry has a long history of greenwashing, using vague language and misleading marketing to suggest that their efforts in renewable energy are more substantial than they really are. For example, while BP (British Petroleum) rebranded itself as "Beyond Petroleum" in the early 2000s, it continued to invest heavily in oil exploration, with only token investments in cleaner technologies.

Agribusiness: Industrial Agriculture and Deforestation

Agriculture, especially the industrialized practices of large agribusiness corporations, is another major contributor to environmental degradation. Industrial agriculture is responsible for widespread deforestation, soil erosion, water contamination, and the loss of biodiversity. Global agricultural giants such as **Cargill, Monsanto (now part of Bayer), Tyson Foods, and JBS** are central players in this issue.

One of the most devastating impacts of industrial agriculture is its contribution to deforestation, particularly in tropical regions like the Amazon rainforest. Cargill, for example, has been linked to the destruction of large swathes of the Amazon through its operations in soy production and cattle farming. Soybeans—largely produced for animal feed and biofuels—are one of the largest drivers of deforestation in the Amazon. The land cleared for soy plantations not only destroys valuable ecosystems but also releases large amounts of carbon dioxide into the atmosphere, further fueling climate change.

Cattle ranching is another key driver of deforestation. In countries like Brazil, large meat producers such as JBS and Brazil Foods (now BRF) are responsible for the clearing of vast areas of forest to make way for cattle pastures. In addition to deforestation, cattle farming is a major source of methane emissions, a potent greenhouse gas. As these companies expand their operations into previously untouched regions, they continue to contribute to environmental degradation on an unprecedented scale.

Industrial agriculture also relies heavily on the use of chemical pesticides, fertilizers, and herbicides, which contribute to water pollution, soil degradation, and the destruction of ecosystems. The widespread use of genetically modified crops (GMOs) by companies like Monsanto has been linked to the decline of pollinator populations, particularly bees, which are crucial for the pollination of many crops.

Even when corporations claim to adopt sustainable practices, such as using "organic" or "sustainable" labels, the scale of industrial agriculture often undermines any meaningful environmental benefits. For example, large organic farming operations may still contribute to soil erosion and water depletion, as they rely on monocultures and excessive irrigation to maintain high yields.

Fast Fashion: The Environmental Toll of Clothing Production

Another example of corporate environmental harm is the fast fashion industry. Major clothing brands like **H&M, Zara, Uniqlo, and Nike** produce clothing at a rapid pace, following trends that change with the seasons. This "throwaway" culture encourages consumers to buy more, wear it less, and discard it quickly, leading to an immense environmental footprint.

The fast fashion industry is notorious for **massive waste, pollution, and exploitation of workers.** The production process involves the use of synthetic fabrics made from petrochemicals, such as polyester and nylon, which shed microplastics into the oceans when washed. The dyeing process alone uses toxic chemicals that pollute water sources. For example, in China, a major textile manufacturing hub, the textile industry has been responsible for polluting over 70% of the country's rivers with dyes and chemicals.

Fast fashion companies are also responsible for creating a disposable culture of cheap, low-quality garments that are worn a handful of times before being discarded. Globally, around **92 million tons of textile waste** is generated each year, with much of it ending up in landfills or incinerators. Despite efforts from some brands to promote sustainability, the fast fashion model is fundamentally unsustainable due to the overconsumption of resources, excessive waste, and labor exploitation in low-wage countries.

Even when companies attempt to pivot toward more sustainable practices, such as producing garments from recycled materials or pledging to reduce carbon footprints, they often fail to address the root causes of their environmental impact—namely, the culture of mass production and overconsumption that lies at the heart of the fast fashion business model.

Technology Companies: E-Waste and Resource Extraction

Technology companies, which are often seen as leaders in innovation and sustainability, also have a significant role in environmental degradation. The rapid pace of technological advancement, combined with the short lifespan of many electronic products, has led to a growing e-waste crisis. Brands like **Apple, Samsung, and Dell** are responsible for the production of millions of devices, such as smartphones, laptops, and tablets, which are frequently discarded as consumers upgrade to newer models.

The extraction of raw materials for these devices, such as coltan, lithium, cobalt, and rare earth metals, often takes place in regions with little regard for environmental protections. Mining operations in places like the Democratic Republic of Congo (where cobalt is mined) have been linked to **soil contamination, water pollution**, and **human rights abuses.** The demand for these metals is set to increase as the world moves toward electric vehicles and renewable energy storage, creating even more pressure on the environment.

The disposal of e-waste is equally problematic. Only about 20% of global e-waste is properly recycled, with the rest being **dumped in landfills or illegally exported to developing countries**, where it contributes to soil and water contamination, as well as the exploitation of vulnerable workers.

Greenwashing: The Corporate Smokescreen

While many corporations are responsible for significant environmental damage, some attempt to position themselves as environmentally friendly through greenwashing—the practice of making misleading or superficial claims about environmental responsibility. Greenwashing is particularly pervasive in industries like fashion, food, and cosmetics, where companies often market their products as "eco-friendly" or "sustainable" without making substantial changes to their core operations.

For example, **Coca-Cola** has long touted its commitment to sustainability by promoting its use of recyclable packaging and water conservation efforts. However, the company continues to produce billions of single-use plastic bottles every year, contributing significantly to the global plastic pollution crisis. Similarly, **H&M** promotes its "Conscious" collection, which claims to use more sustainable materials, but continues to rely on the fast fashion model, with cheap production and rapid turnover of clothing that contributes to environmental degradation.

By focusing on marketing and public relations campaigns rather than making meaningful, systemic changes, companies engage in greenwashing to deflect criticism and maintain their profits while avoiding the real responsibility of transforming their operations for sustainability.

The role of large corporations in environmental degradation cannot be underestimated. Whether through the burning of **fossil fuels, the destruction of natural ecosystems, the promotion of unsustainable consumption**, or the spread of misinformation through greenwashing, these entities have prioritized profit over the planet. While some companies have made efforts to adopt more sustainable practices, the reality is that much more needs to be done to align corporate operations with the health of the Earth. As consumers, investors, and citizens, we must hold corporations accountable, demand transparency, and push for systemic change that prioritizes the long-term health of our planet over short-term financial gain.

While the general patterns of environmental harm caused by large corporations have been clearly identified, it's the specific, often catastrophic, actions of these corporations that reveal the full scale of the problem. From the destruction of critical ecosystems to the **poisoning of communities,** the actions of certain corporations have pushed our planet to the brink. These corporations, driven by profit motives and a relentless focus on growth, have often disregarded the long-term environmental and social consequences of their operations. In this section, we will examine several high-profile examples of corporate harm, illustrating the devastating effects of corporate greed.

1. ExxonMobil: Climate Change Denial and Environmental Contamination

One of the most notorious examples of corporate harm is ExxonMobil, one of the world's largest oil companies. **ExxonMobil has been at the center of not just environmental degradation but also climate change denial and misinformation campaigns.** In the 1970s, Exxon scientists were some of the first to confirm the link between fossil fuel emissions and global warming. However, instead of acting on this knowledge, **the company spent decades suppressing scientific findings, funding climate denial think tanks, and launching misleading advertising campaigns to downplay the seriousness of climate change.**

In addition to its role in climate change, **ExxonMobil has been directly responsible for multiple environmental disasters,** including the infamous Exxon Valdez oil spill in 1989. The spill released 11 million gallons of crude oil into Alaska's Prince William Sound, causing one of the most devastating environmental catastrophes in history. It killed thousands of marine animals, destroyed ecosystems, and caused long-lasting damage to local communities, including indigenous groups who rely on fishing for their livelihoods. Despite ExxonMobil's promises to clean up and compensate for the damage, the impact of the spill is still being felt more than three decades later.

In recent years, ExxonMobil has faced numerous lawsuits for its role in exacerbating climate change and failing to disclose the environmental risks of its business operations. The company's continued pursuit of fossil fuel extraction, particularly through **fracking, has also been linked to water contamination, earthquakes, and methane emissions—** all of which have significant long-term consequences for local ecosystems and human health.

2. Monsanto (Bayer): The Roundup Controversy and Agricultural Chemicals

Monsanto, now owned by Bayer, has long been one of the most influential—and controversial—companies in the world of agriculture. Monsanto is infamous for its **genetically modified organisms (GMOs)**, including the creation of Roundup—a weed killer that became the most widely used herbicide in the world. However, Monsanto's legacy is far from a simple story of innovation and agricultural success. The company has been **repeatedly accused of toxic contamination, environmental harm, and corporate malfeasance.**

The most notable controversy surrounding Monsanto involves the herbicide glyphosate, the active ingredient in Roundup. Studies have shown that glyphosate is a probable human carcinogen, with strong links to non-Hodgkin's lymphoma. In 2018, Monsanto/Bayer was ordered to pay $289 million in damages to a groundskeeper who developed cancer after prolonged exposure to the herbicide. Glyphosate is widely used in farming, but its overuse has led to resistant superweeds, which in turn has led to more **toxic herbicides** being sprayed on crops.

Additionally, Monsanto has been accused of unethical practices related to its patent enforcement. The company **aggressively pursues lawsuits** against farmers whose crops become contaminated with Monsanto's patented genetically modified seeds, even when the contamination happens through no fault of the farmers themselves. These lawsuits have resulted in the **loss of family farms and significant financial distress for agricultural communities across the United States and beyond.**

Monsanto's aggressive use of biotechnology has also contributed to the biodiversity crisis. The company's genetically modified crops often rely on **monoculture farming**, which depletes soil quality, reduces genetic diversity, and makes crops more vulnerable to pests and diseases. This model of farming, driven by Monsanto's GMO seeds, is one of the reasons for the widespread loss of soil fertility and the collapse of pollinator populations like bees.

3. Amazon: Deforestation, Worker Exploitation, and Unsustainable Practices

As the world's largest online retailer, Amazon has been a driving force in the global economy, providing convenience for millions of consumers. However, its business practices have wreaked havoc on both the environment and workers, exposing the dark side of e-commerce and mass consumption. Amazon's environmental impact is profound, especially when it comes to deforestation and resource depletion.

The company has been linked to **large-scale deforestation** in Brazil, where it sources paper, packaging, and other materials. Amazon's vast global logistics network requires enormous quantities of packaging, and much of this packaging comes from unsustainable sources that contribute to forest destruction. Furthermore, Amazon has faced criticism for selling products that are directly linked to environmental destruction, such as products made from **illegal timber, palm oil, and other commodities tied to deforestation.**

In addition to its environmental footprint, Amazon has been criticized for its **treatment of workers** and its contribution to the **consumer culture of waste**. Amazon's vast distribution centers, which rely on fast shipping and high turnover rates, often subject workers to harsh conditions, including long hours, low pay, and the pressure to meet impossible targets. Meanwhile, the company's aggressive push for same-day delivery and mass consumption has led to a **massive increase in packaging waste, much of which is non-recyclable.**

Despite Amazon's claims of commitment to sustainability, its actions often tell a different story. The company has pledged to become carbon neutral by 2040, but it continues to build massive warehouses and data centers that require **significant energy consumption,** much of it sourced from non-renewable fossil fuels. Additionally, the carbon emissions from its shipping network and the life-cycle impact of the products it sells are far from being fully offset by the company's sustainability efforts.

4. Nestlé: Water Privatization and Environmental Exploitation

The multinational food and beverage company Nestlé has long been embroiled in controversies surrounding its water extraction practices, which have contributed to **water shortages** in many regions around the world. Nestlé has been criticized for extracting water from public aquifers and selling it as bottled water in areas suffering from droughts and water scarcity.

In California, for instance, Nestlé has been extracting water from springs in the San Bernardino Mountains, using a **permit that expired more than two decades ago.** Despite facing protests from local communities and environmental groups, the company continued to bottle water and sell it at a profit. In 2020, Nestlé sold its North American water division to a private equity firm, but not before facing growing backlash over its exploitation of public water resources.

Nestlé has also been accused of contributing to plastic pollution. The company produces **billions of plastic bottles every year**, much of which ends up in landfills, oceans, and rivers. Despite some efforts to reduce plastic waste and promote recyclable packaging, Nestlé remains one of the **largest plastic polluters in the world**. In 2020, Nestlé, alongside other major companies like Coca-Cola and Pepsi, was ranked as one of the top producers of plastic waste in a report by **Break Free From Plastic**.

5. Shell: Oil Spills and Environmental Injustice

Royal Dutch Shell, one of the largest oil companies globally, has been responsible for multiple environmental disasters, most notably the 1990s oil spills in Nigeria and the Deepwater Horizon oil spill in 2010. These incidents underscore the company's long history of environmental irresponsibility and its unwillingness to fully embrace sustainable practices.

The Shell oil spill in the Niger Delta has devastated the environment and local communities for decades. Nigeria's Ogoni people, in particular, have suffered from oil-related pollution in their lands, which has destroyed local ecosystems, contaminated drinking water sources, and caused severe health problems. Shell has been accused of covering up the extent of the damage and delaying efforts to clean up the contamination. Despite international pressure, Shell has continued to operate in the region, facing minimal regulatory accountability for the widespread environmental and human costs of its activities.

The Deepwater Horizon oil spill off the coast of Louisiana in 2010 resulted in the release of nearly 5 million barrels of oil into the Gulf of Mexico, creating one of the worst environmental disasters in U.S. history. The spill killed marine life, destroyed habitats, and caused irreparable damage to local fishing industries. Despite being fined billions of dollars and facing public outrage, Shell and its partners did little to change the way they operate, continuing to drill in environmentally sensitive areas with a focus on maximizing profits rather than prioritizing safety and sustainability.

Large corporations, whether in fossil fuels, agriculture, retail, or food and beverage industries, are contributing to widespread environmental harm that affects ecosystems, communities, and future generations. These corporations are driven by short-term profit motives, often at the expense of the long-term health of the planet. While some companies have made half-hearted attempts at reform or embraced greenwashing tactics to improve their public image, their core practices and priorities remain deeply entrenched in environmental destruction.

To address this issue, **systemic change is required**—not only in corporate practices but also in how we, as consumers, demand greater accountability from these global giants. Public pressure, stronger regulations, and collective action are essential to forcing corporations to align their operations with the urgent needs of a sustainable and just world.

Corporate Lobbying and Legislation Blockage

The environmental damage caused by large corporations is not limited to their direct actions. One of the most insidious ways corporations obstruct progress toward sustainability is through their influence over political systems, particularly in the form of corporate lobbying and the blockage of environmental legislation. By leveraging financial power, influence, and a network of well-placed advocates, **these corporations have been able to delay, dilute, or outright block meaningful policies designed to protect the environment.** This section explores how corporate lobbying has become a major roadblock to environmental progress and the ways in which specific industries have successfully **manipulated legislation for their benefit.**

1. The Fossil Fuel Industry's Stranglehold on Climate Policy

The fossil fuel industry is perhaps the most powerful corporate sector when it comes to blocking environmental legislation. As the primary driver of global warming, this industry's profits depend heavily on fossil fuel extraction, and they have spent billions of dollars in recent decades to influence public policy and protect their interests.

At the heart of the fossil fuel industry's influence is its ability to lobby politicians to delay or weaken climate-related legislation. **The American Petroleum Institute (API)**, a trade association representing major oil and gas companies like **ExxonMobil, Chevron, and Shell, is one of the most active lobbying forces in Washington, D.C.** The API has spent hundreds of millions of dollars over the years to prevent stronger climate regulations, including efforts to block carbon taxes, weaken air quality standards, and roll back restrictions on greenhouse gas emissions. In fact, **ExxonMobil alone has spent more than $200 million lobbying** U.S. policymakers over the past decade to influence energy policy, including efforts to defeat carbon pricing proposals.

One of the most glaring examples of corporate influence is the Paris Climate Agreement negotiations, where the fossil fuel lobby exerted significant pressure on politicians to weaken commitments to reduce greenhouse gas emissions. In 2017, **when President**

Donald Trump announced the United States' withdrawal from the agreement, it was widely seen as a victory for the fossil fuel industry, which had been pushing for fewer international constraints on carbon emissions. Many oil and gas companies actively opposed climate action and funded organizations that undermined the science behind climate change.

The fossil fuel industry's influence extends beyond lobbying. It often works in tandem with think tanks like the **Cato Institute** and the **Heartland Institute, which spread misinformation and question the validity of climate science.** These organizations are funded by corporations like ExxonMobil and Chevron, and they have played a critical role in manufacturing doubt about the reality of climate change. Their efforts to discredit the scientific consensus on climate change have delayed political action for decades, allowing corporations to continue extracting and burning fossil fuels without facing consequences.

2. Agricultural Lobbying: Defending Destructive Practices

The agricultural sector, especially large agribusiness corporations, has been just as successful in blocking meaningful environmental legislation. **Cargill, Tyson Foods, Monsanto (now part of Bayer), and ADM (Archer Daniels Midland)** have enormous financial clout and political influence, particularly in the United States, where farm subsidies and agricultural policies are deeply entrenched.

Monsanto, for instance, has used its **lobbying power to push for the deregulation of genetically modified organisms (GMOs)** and the widespread use of pesticides and herbicides like glyphosate. Despite mounting **evidence linking glyphosate to cancer,** Monsanto has been able to block stronger regulations and has aggressively campaigned to prevent restrictions on its use. The company also played a key role in pushing for the **Biotechnology Regulatory Transparency Act in 2013, which would have prevented states from passing their own laws regarding GMO labeling.**

Beyond GMOs, agribusinesses have lobbied to protect subsidies for industrial agriculture, which is heavily reliant on **monocultures, synthetic fertilizers, and pesticides.** This system contributes to **environmental degradation**, including soil erosion, water pollution, and biodiversity loss. Despite the environmental toll of industrial farming, farm subsidies continue to prop up large agribusinesses, encouraging **unsustainable practices. The Farm Bill** in the U.S. is an example of legislation repeatedly shaped by agribusiness lobbying, as **it directs billions of dollars in subsidies toward crop insurance**, price supports for commodity crops like corn and soybeans, and financial support for biofuels, all of which **contribute to the continuation of environmentally harmful practices.**

Large agribusiness corporations also work to block stronger environmental regulations at the state level. For instance, Cargill has been involved in **lobbying efforts to prevent states from passing laws that would protect workers' rights,** reduce the use of harmful chemicals, or promote sustainable farming practices. In the case of animal welfare laws, major companies like Tyson Foods and JBS have actively opposed reforms aimed at improving the conditions of factory-farmed animals, even though these practices contribute to pollution and health risks.

3. The Role of the Pharmaceutical Industry in Blocking Health and Environmental Legislation

While the pharmaceutical industry is often associated with public health concerns, it also has a significant role in environmental degradation. Major pharmaceutical companies have been known to lobby against environmental regulations that would limit the environmental harm caused by their products, particularly with regard to chemical pollutants.

Pharmaceutical companies manufacture and release **millions of tons of chemicals into the environment** through the production process, the disposal of expired medications, and the accumulation of pharmaceutical waste in water systems. Hormonal medications, for example, are among the most common pharmaceutical **contaminants found in waterways**, where they disrupt local ecosystems by interfering with the endocrine systems of wildlife. Despite evidence that certain pharmaceutical chemicals pose a risk to both human health and biodiversity, pharmaceutical giants like **Pfizer, Johnson & Johnson, and Merck** have successfully lobbied against regulatory measures to limit the environmental impact of their products.

For example, in the European Union, the pharmaceutical industry has pushed back against proposed regulations that would require companies to test their products for potential environmental effects before they reach the market. In the United States, the industry has been successful in blocking federal oversight of pharmaceutical waste disposal, which **continues to pollute the environment and compromise public health.**

4. The Tech Industry: E-Waste and Resource Extraction

The tech industry—led by companies like **Apple, Google, and Samsung**—has also become a major player in lobbying against environmental legislation, particularly in the areas of electronic waste (e-waste) and resource extraction. As the demand for smartphones, laptops, and other electronic devices has skyrocketed, so has the electronic waste crisis, with millions of tons of discarded electronics ending up in landfills or being shipped to developing countries, where they often pose significant environmental and health risks.

Despite growing concerns over the toxic components in electronic devices (such as lead, mercury, and cadmium), tech companies have lobbied to delay or weaken legislation that would require extended producer responsibility (EPR) for e-waste recycling. Apple, for example, has been criticized for lobbying against state-level legislation in the U.S. that would require it to take responsibility for the recycling of its products. In India, tech companies have lobbied the government to delay the implementation of laws that would limit the export of hazardous e-waste from developed nations.

Furthermore, the tech industry's reliance on rare earth metals—which are often mined under environmentally devastating conditions—has led to extensive lobbying to weaken regulations around mining practices. Companies like **Apple and Tesla** have come under fire for sourcing materials like lithium and cobalt from countries with lax environmental protections. While these materials are critical for the production of smartphones, electric car batteries, and other high-tech products, the environmental and social consequences of their extraction are often ignored in favor of lower production costs.

5. The Role of Lobbyists and Think Tanks in Blocking Green Legislation

Corporate lobbying is not just about direct influence on politicians; it also involves the use of think tanks, lobbying firms, and third-party organizations that work to shape public opinion and influence legislative agendas. These organizations often present themselves as independent and nonpartisan but are funded by corporations seeking to block or delay environmental regulations.

For example, the **American Legislative Exchange Council (ALEC)**, a nonprofit that drafts model legislation for state lawmakers, has long been a key player in promoting corporate interests in the United States. **ALEC has received significant funding from fossil fuel companies** and has been behind efforts to block carbon taxes, reduce funding for renewable energy programs, and deregulate the energy sector.

Similarly, groups like the **Competitive Enterprise Institute and the Heartland Institute, both of which receive funding from the fossil fuel and tobacco industries**, have been central in spreading misinformation about climate change and opposing climate action. These organizations serve as powerful vehicles for corporate interests, pushing narratives that undermine the science behind climate change and advocating for free-market solutions that often ignore the environmental costs of industrial activity.

The influence of corporate lobbying on environmental legislation is a profound barrier to meaningful progress in addressing the climate crisis and environmental degradation. Whether it's fossil fuel giants blocking carbon taxes, agribusinesses protecting unsustainable farming practices, or pharmaceutical companies undermining regulations on toxic chemicals, **these corporations are actively working to delay the policies we need to protect the planet.** This section underscores the necessity of tackling corporate lobbying and ensuring that politicians are held accountable for their role in obstructing environmental protection. We must demand stronger regulations, promote transparency in lobbying, and recognize that true environmental justice can only be achieved when corporate power is reined in and public interest is placed at the forefront of policymaking.

Greenwashing and Corporate Malfeasance

While direct environmental destruction through resource extraction, pollution, and unsustainable practices is undoubtedly harmful, a more insidious form of corporate harm has emerged in the last few decades: greenwashing. This tactic, in which companies market themselves as environmentally friendly or sustainable without making significant changes to their core business practices, is not only misleading but also actively prevents real environmental progress. Greenwashing allows corporations to maintain their profits while giving the illusion of environmental responsibility, all the while continuing to engage in activities that contribute to ecological degradation.

1. The Rise of Greenwashing: Deceptive Marketing and False Claims

Greenwashing is a term coined to describe the practice of deceptively portraying an organization's products, services, or practices as environmentally friendly when, in reality, they are not. This often involves the use of vague or misleading claims about sustainability, such as labeling products as "eco-friendly," "natural," or "green," without providing clear definitions or third-party verification. Companies that engage in greenwashing often do so to capitalize on the growing consumer demand for environmentally responsible products, without making the necessary changes to their operations to back up those claims.

The scope of greenwashing is vast, with companies across nearly every industry—from fashion to food to energy—engaging in the practice. In the fashion industry, for example, companies will often tout their use of "sustainable materials" or "eco-friendly" dyes, while continuing to rely on fast fashion models that encourage mass production, cheap labor, and unethical supply chains that exploit workers and harm the environment. The industry is one of the largest polluters globally, yet many fashion giants use greenwashing techniques to mask their harmful environmental impact.

Similarly, the food industry has witnessed a surge of companies claiming to adopt "sustainable sourcing" or "zero waste" practices, while their business models remain deeply unsustainable. Companies like Nestlé and **Coca-Cola** frequently boast about their environmental efforts in marketing campaigns, only to have those claims debunked later. For instance, **Nestlé** has publicly promoted its efforts to use "sustainably sourced palm oil," but the company's palm oil supply chain is directly linked to deforestation in sensitive ecosystems like those in Indonesia and Malaysia. These contradictions expose the manipulation at the heart of greenwashing.

The term "greenwashing" also applies to corporate behavior in industries like energy and automotive. Companies like BP and Shell, which are responsible for massive levels of environmental pollution through their continued extraction and burning of fossil fuels, have spent millions on advertising campaigns to brand themselves as "green energy" companies. Their public relations efforts often focus on investments in renewable energy or carbon capture technologies, yet the overwhelming majority of their revenues still come from fossil fuels. This **strategy is designed to distract from their true environmental record, which includes catastrophic spills, the exacerbation of climate change, and resistance to policies that would effectively curb carbon emissions.**

2. The Deceptive Claims: Examples of Greenwashing

One of the most flagrant examples of greenwashing is the practice of labeling products as "carbon neutral" or "climate-positive" without any meaningful change to the company's overall carbon footprint. For example, **IKEA** has been celebrated for its commitments to reducing carbon emissions, but the company still relies on unsustainable sourcing of materials like wood and plastic. The company's investments in sustainable products are often overshadowed by its continued reliance on mass production, overconsumption, and long supply chains, which all contribute to its overall environmental footprint.

Another notorious example of greenwashing comes from the automotive industry, with companies like **Volkswagen and General Motors** claiming to be "leaders in green technology" through the introduction of electric vehicles (EVs). While these companies have indeed made strides toward EV production, their previous environmental actions tell a different story. **Volkswagen's** infamous "dieselgate" scandal, where the company installed software to cheat emissions tests, was a **clear demonstration of its disregard for environmental regulations and the public's trust.** Similarly, GM, despite promoting its electric vehicle lineup, has lobbied against stricter emissions regulations in the United States for decades, focusing on the continued production of gas-guzzling vehicles and SUVs.

BP (British Petroleum) has long been a leader in the greenwashing game. In 2000, the company rebranded itself as "Beyond Petroleum," signaling its shift towards renewable energy. However, despite the name change and its marketing campaign to promote "green" energy solutions, the company's investment in renewable sources remained marginal compared to its massive profits from oil and gas exploration. **BP has been responsible for some of the worst environmental disasters in history,** including the Deepwater Horizon oil spill in 2010, and its commitment to transitioning away from fossil fuels has been widely seen as insufficient and symbolic at best. BP's greenwashing efforts are a stark example of how corporate giants attempt to reframe their image without making substantive changes to their core operations.

3. Consequences of Greenwashing: The Erosion of Trust and Delayed Progress

Greenwashing does not only mislead consumers, it also undermines real efforts to combat climate change. When companies make false or exaggerated claims about their sustainability efforts, they divert attention away from genuine solutions and delay progress towards real environmental change. Consumers, believing they are supporting responsible companies, continue to purchase harmful products that contribute to environmental destruction. The false sense of progress that greenwashing creates also weakens the pressure on governments and corporations to take more substantial actions toward reducing carbon emissions and promoting sustainability.

Moreover, greenwashing fosters a culture of complacency. By showcasing minor environmental improvements without addressing the deeper, more systemic problems, corporations allow society to believe that they are making meaningful changes when they are not. This not only undermines public trust in companies but also in the very idea of corporate responsibility. As a result, meaningful environmental policies may be delayed or dismissed, because consumers and legislators feel that the private sector is already doing enough. The consequences of this phenomenon are particularly dangerous as the climate crisis accelerates and the window for action narrows.

4. Combatting Greenwashing: What Consumers and Citizens Can Do

To tackle greenwashing effectively, consumers, governments, and environmental organizations must hold companies accountable and demand transparency. Consumers can start by educating themselves on what constitutes a truly sustainable product. Look for certifications like **Fair Trade, B Corp, and Energy Star**, which are independently verified, and be wary of vague claims like "eco-friendly" or "green" without proof.

Consumers can also push back by supporting companies that are genuinely committed to sustainability and demanding more from those who engage in greenwashing. When corporations hear from their customers, they are more likely to act. It is essential to pressure corporations to commit to transparent reporting on their environmental impacts, including not only their green initiatives but also their overall environmental footprint.

Governments must also take a stronger stance in regulating corporate claims and holding companies accountable for their environmental promises. Stricter laws should be enforced to prevent false advertising and ensure that companies back up their sustainability claims with verifiable actions. In the European Union, for instance, the **EU Green Deal** is attempting to address such issues by setting binding sustainability targets, but enforcement mechanisms are needed to close loopholes and combat greenwashing on a global scale.

From direct environmental destruction through unsustainable practices to greenwashing and lobbying efforts aimed at blocking or weakening legislation, large corporations have proven to be formidable barriers to progress. Yet, despite these challenges, there is hope.

By holding corporations accountable—whether through demanding better transparency, pushing for stronger regulations, or choosing products and companies that genuinely prioritize sustainability—consumers and citizens can begin to shift the balance of power. Ultimately, the fight for the planet's future is not just against polluting industries but also against the entrenched interests that seek to perpetuate environmental harm for profit. If we want to build a sustainable, just world, it is crucial that we challenge the power of corporations, expose their greenwashing tactics, and push for real, systemic change.

Chapter 3

Greenwashing – The Corporate Smokescreen

In recent years, the term "greenwashing" has become increasingly common in discussions about environmental responsibility, but what exactly does it mean? At its core, greenwashing refers to the practice in which corporations or organizations deceive consumers by making false or exaggerated claims about the environmental benefits of their products, services, or operations. This deliberate misrepresentation can take many forms, from using misleading labels and advertising slogans to creating false narratives about sustainability and environmental stewardship. The goal of greenwashing is simple: to capitalize on growing consumer demand for environmentally friendly products and practices without actually making meaningful changes to reduce environmental harm.

While greenwashing might seem like a new buzzword, it has roots in much older practices of corporate manipulation. The phenomenon is tied to the realization that sustainability has become a major selling point for companies. As consumers become more environmentally conscious, they are increasingly seeking out brands that reflect their values—ones that promise to protect natural resources, reduce carbon emissions, and offer products that are safer for both people and the planet. However, many corporations have realized that they can simply appear to be environmentally responsible without undergoing the costly and complex processes of actually changing their operations or business models.

Greenwashing is a form of environmental deception—it's not just about minor embellishments or an occasional oversell of benefits; it's an intentional attempt to mislead the public. The problem with this practice is not only its dishonesty but also its potential to derail genuine efforts to solve environmental problems. When consumers are misled by companies that claim to be "eco-friendly" or "sustainable," they may feel less motivated to make the necessary lifestyle changes or support organizations and initiatives that are truly making a difference.

The Scope of Greenwashing: How Big Is the Problem?

Greenwashing affects almost every industry, and its scale has grown significantly in recent years as environmental awareness has risen. The fashion industry, food industry, energy sector, automotive companies, and even tech giants have been caught in the act of greenwashing. A 2021 report by the **European Commission** found that up to 40% of environmental claims made by companies online could be misleading or false. In particular, companies in high-emission industries—such as oil, mining, and agriculture—have been particularly aggressive in using greenwashing as a public relations tool to deflect criticism of their environmental practices.

The sheer scale of greenwashing has made it difficult for consumers to distinguish between genuinely sustainable brands and those that are merely adopting "green" rhetoric for financial gain. A 2019 survey by the **Consumer Reports** found that nearly two-thirds of Americans said they were more likely to buy products from companies that advertise themselves as environmentally responsible, but fewer than 1 in 10 could accurately identify whether these companies were, in fact, making real strides toward sustainability. This gap in consumer understanding is exactly what greenwashing aims to exploit.

Despite the increasing prevalence of greenwashing, it remains largely unregulated. While some countries have begun to implement stricter laws on misleading environmental claims, there is still no universal standard for what constitutes a legitimate environmental claim or what should be classified as greenwashing. As a result, companies are free to make vague or unsubstantiated claims, such as stating that a product is "eco-friendly" or "natural" without needing to provide any meaningful evidence.

How Greenwashing Works: Tactics and Techniques

Greenwashing can take many forms, but several common tactics are used by companies to present themselves as more environmentally responsible than they actually are. These tactics often rely on vague language, selective use of facts, and deceptive visuals that play on consumers' increasing environmental awareness.

1.	**Vague	or	Unverifiable	Claims**
One of the most common tactics in greenwashing is the use of vague terms like "green," "eco-friendly," "natural," or "sustainable." These terms are inherently subjective and often lack clear definitions, which allows companies to use them without providing concrete proof. For example, a company might claim that its packaging is "environmentally friendly" without specifying how it was produced, what materials were used, or whether it is recyclable. The term "natural" is similarly ambiguous, and it can be used to imply that a product is better for the environment without backing up the claim with specific evidence.

2.	**Misleading	Certifications	and	Labels**
Another greenwashing strategy involves the use of logos or labels that suggest a product has been certified by an independent environmental organization. While some **certification programs are legitimate and trustworthy (such as Fair Trade, Energy Star, or Forest Stewardship Council),** others may be created or sponsored by the companies themselves or may lack rigorous standards. A product with a label like "green certified" or "eco-safe" may look like it meets specific environmental standards, but it could be the result of a company creating its own certification with little to no oversight.

3.	**Selective	Disclosure**
Companies often use selective disclosure to highlight one small environmentally friendly

aspect of their product while ignoring broader environmental issues that may overshadow their efforts. For example, a company might advertise its use of recycled materials in one product line, but fail to disclose that most of its other products are made with unsustainable resources or that their manufacturing process is still extremely polluting. This selective highlighting of a product's green features while downplaying its negative impact is a key tactic in greenwashing.

4.   False   or   Exaggerated   Environmental   Claims
Companies may also use outright false or exaggerated environmental claims. For example, a company may claim that its product is "carbon neutral" or that it has a "zero-waste" production process when, in reality, the company is only making minor improvements in one area while continuing to engage in harmful practices elsewhere. One of the most notorious examples of this is the concept of "carbon neutrality," where companies claim to offset their emissions by investing in carbon credit schemes without actually reducing the emissions they are producing. Often, these offsets are poorly managed or have no measurable environmental benefit.

5.   Distracting   from   Larger   Issues
Some companies engage in distraction tactics by pointing to their small, isolated actions while ignoring the larger, systemic issues they contribute to. For instance, a company might promote a small, "green" initiative, like planting a few trees or reducing plastic waste in one specific product line, while continuing to engage in highly damaging practices such as deforestation, unsustainable resource extraction, or mass production of disposable goods. By focusing on a single positive action, companies divert attention from their overall environmental footprint.

Greenwashing is not merely an inconvenient marketing trend; it is a direct hindrance to the kind of systemic change that is urgently needed to address the world's environmental crises. By making it difficult for consumers to differentiate between companies that are genuinely committed to sustainability and those that are only interested in appearing eco-friendly, greenwashing undermines both public trust and collective action.

It is not enough for consumers to demand that companies become more sustainable; we must also demand accountability, transparency, and real, verifiable change. Understanding the techniques of greenwashing is the first step in recognizing when companies are trying to exploit our desire for environmental responsibility for their own gain. By recognizing and calling out greenwashing for what it is—a smokescreen that distracts from true environmental action—we can move closer to a world where corporate accountability and environmental stewardship go hand in hand.

While greenwashing can be subtle and difficult to spot, some companies have taken it to new extremes. In this section, we'll explore some of the most egregious examples of greenwashing across different industries—ranging from fashion to energy to food—highlighting how companies manipulate their environmental claims to mislead consumers and obscure their true impact on the planet. These cases illustrate how greenwashing is used not only to deceive but to stall real environmental progress by diverting attention and resources away from meaningful change.

1. The Fashion Industry: Fast Fashion's "Sustainable" Lie

One of the most well-known industries associated with greenwashing is fashion. The rise of fast fashion has led to a global environmental crisis: massive water consumption, pollution, and waste. Yet, many major clothing brands have recently rebranded themselves as "sustainable" or "eco-friendly" to appeal to increasingly conscientious consumers. But a closer look reveals that most of these claims are little more than marketing gimmicks designed to protect profits while **perpetuating environmentally harmful practices**.

H&M is a prime example. The company launched its "Conscious Collection", claiming to use more sustainable materials like organic cotton and recycled fabrics. Yet, despite these claims, the company's fast fashion model—which encourages rapid production, low-cost labor, and short product lifecycles—remains unchanged. In fact, an investigation by the New York Times revealed that even the recycled materials used in the Conscious Collection often had minimal environmental impact because of the way the garments were produced. H&M continues to produce massive volumes of clothing, creating a cycle of overconsumption and waste, while promoting the idea that a few "green" pieces can absolve the brand's overall environmental impact.

Another greenwashing example is **Zara**, a company owned by the Spanish retail giant Inditex. Zara has marketed its "Join Life" collection as being more sustainable, using materials such as organic cotton and recycled polyester. However, the collection accounts for only a small portion of Zara's overall production, and the company's broader business model of "cheap, disposable fashion" is inherently unsustainable. As **Environmental Justice Foundation** reports, the fashion industry is responsible for 10% of global carbon emissions—a number that fast fashion brands like Zara are not addressing through these limited initiatives. This creates a dangerous illusion of responsibility without addressing the root cause: overproduction and overconsumption.

2. The Food Industry: Misleading Labels and Sustainability Claims

The food industry has also been rife with greenwashing, especially as consumers increasingly demand transparency and sustainability. Companies in this sector often advertise their products as "natural," "organic," or "sustainable," even when their production methods remain far from environmentally friendly.

Nestlé, one of the largest food and beverage companies in the world, is often cited for greenwashing. In 2020, Nestlé launched an advertising campaign touting its commitment to sustainable practices, particularly the reduction of plastic waste and packaging. The company claimed that it was working towards a 100% recyclable packaging goal and was investing in new recycling technologies. However, Nestlé is one of the largest producers of single-use plastic in the world, contributing massively to global plastic pollution.

Despite its claims, the company continues to produce billions of plastic bottles, much of which ends up in landfills or the ocean. In fact, a report by the environmental group Greenpeace found that **Nestlé, along with Coca-Cola and PepsiCo, was responsible for producing the most plastic waste globally**.

Similarly, Coca-Cola has marketed itself as environmentally responsible by claiming it is "working toward a world without waste" and launching initiatives aimed at increasing the recyclability of its products. However, Coca-Cola continues to sell billions of plastic bottles worldwide. These bottles, which often do not get properly recycled, contribute massively to ocean pollution. Coca-Cola's claims of being environmentally friendly ring hollow when considering the overwhelming impact of its plastic production, which remains a primary contributor to global pollution.

Another example is **Chobani**, a major yogurt brand that has marketed its products as "all-natural" and "sustainable." While Chobani has made some improvements, such as switching to non-GMO ingredients and using more sustainable packaging, the company has faced criticism for sourcing milk from large industrial farms that contribute to environmental degradation, including water contamination, greenhouse gas emissions, and excessive land use. In addition, the company's use of plastic containers is a major contributor to plastic waste. Despite these concerns, Chobani continues to advertise its products as eco-friendly, with little attention given to the broader, systemic issues in the dairy industry.

3. The Automotive Industry: Electric Cars and False Claims

The automotive industry has also been heavily implicated in greenwashing, particularly with the rise of electric vehicles (EVs). While the development of EVs is a positive step toward reducing carbon emissions, several automakers have used greenwashing tactics to obscure the environmental damage their businesses continue to cause.

One infamous example is **Volkswagen**, which has faced widespread backlash over the **"Dieselgate"** scandal. In 2015, it was revealed that Volkswagen had installed software in its diesel vehicles to cheat emissions tests, thereby evading regulations intended to reduce harmful emissions. At the same time, the company had been heavily promoting itself as an eco-conscious brand, with campaigns touting its commitment to "green" technologies and emissions-free driving. This false image of environmental stewardship was shattered by the scandal, revealing how Volkswagen had manipulated emissions data to mislead consumers and regulators. Even after the scandal, Volkswagen continues to market its electric vehicles as environmentally responsible without fully addressing the ongoing environmental harm caused by its internal combustion engine vehicles.

General Motors (GM) is another example of greenwashing in the automotive industry. GM has heavily promoted its electric vehicle (EV) lineup, especially the Chevrolet Bolt, as part of its vision for a sustainable future. However, despite these claims, the company continues to invest heavily in the production of gas-guzzling trucks and SUVs, which make up the bulk of its sales and contribute significantly to carbon emissions. GM has also lobbied against stricter fuel efficiency standards, undermining its public image as a leader in green technology. This selective emphasis on EVs while continuing to prioritize high-emission vehicles is a classic case of greenwashing, where the company creates an illusion of environmental responsibility while failing to address its broader environmental footprint.

4. The Energy Sector: Fossil Fuels and the "Green" Oil Companies

The fossil fuel industry is perhaps the most significant perpetrator of greenwashing. Companies like BP, Shell, and ExxonMobil have long relied on greenwashing to rebrand themselves as environmentally conscious organizations, despite their continued role in causing climate change through the extraction and burning of oil and gas.

BP, for example, once rebranded itself as "Beyond Petroleum" in 2000, signaling a commitment to transitioning to renewable energy. However, over the past two decades, BP has continued to invest billions of dollars in the extraction of fossil fuels, with only a small fraction of its budget going to renewables. The company's "carbon neutral" claims are often dismissed as disingenuous, as they rely on carbon offset projects (which are often ineffective or difficult to verify) rather than reducing emissions at their source. BP's continued environmental destruction through its oil and gas drilling operations directly undermines its green claims.

Shell, similarly, markets itself as a "sustainable" energy provider, boasting investments in wind and solar energy, while its core business remains deeply entrenched in oil and gas extraction. The company's pledges to reduce carbon emissions are undermined by its continued push for new oil and gas exploration and fossil fuel extraction, contributing to environmental degradation at an alarming rate.

Even ExxonMobil has been guilty of greenwashing, claiming that it is actively working toward a "low-carbon future." Yet, ExxonMobil's investments in clean energy technologies have been limited, and its lobbying efforts continue to block or delay meaningful climate policies. The company's reputation as a "green" corporation is inconsistent with its ongoing practices of oil extraction and petroleum production, which are some of the largest contributors to global warming.

These examples of greenwashing demonstrate that corporate efforts to market themselves as environmentally responsible are often little more than disguised public relations campaigns designed to protect their profits without making substantial changes. By utilizing vague claims, misleading certifications, selective disclosures, and false advertising, companies can create an illusion of sustainability while continuing to harm the environment.

As consumers, we must become more vigilant and informed, pushing back against deceptive claims and demanding accountability. At the same time, governments must step up to create stronger regulations that prevent greenwashing and ensure that companies making environmental claims can be held to a high standard of proof.

Greenwashing may be a pervasive problem, but it is not an insurmountable one. By exposing these false narratives and holding corporations accountable, we can encourage real, meaningful progress toward a sustainable future.

How Consumers Can Identify Greenwashing

While greenwashing is a significant issue, consumers are not helpless in the face of corporate manipulation. In fact, by becoming more discerning and educated, we can identify greenwashing tactics and make informed decisions that support true environmental sustainability. Recognizing when companies are "greenwashing" is essential for holding them accountable and pushing them toward genuine environmental responsibility. In this section, we'll explore practical ways to identify greenwashing and how consumers can take action to avoid falling for these misleading claims.

1. Understand Common Greenwashing Terms and Claims

One of the first steps in recognizing greenwashing is understanding the language companies use to make their products sound eco-friendly. Be wary of vague terms such as "green," "natural," "eco-friendly," and "sustainable," which can be used without clear definitions or evidence to support the claims. Without a specific standard or certification to back up these terms, they remain open to interpretation and can easily be exploited by companies hoping to ride the wave of consumer interest in sustainability.

For example, the term "natural" is often used in the beauty, food, and cleaning product industries. However, this doesn't necessarily mean that the product is free from harmful chemicals or that it was produced sustainably. Companies can use this term without offering any proof of the product's impact on the environment, leaving consumers in the dark about what "natural" really means.

2. Look for Certifications and Labels, but Check Their Legitimacy

Legitimate certifications and labels can help guide consumers toward more sustainable products, but not all eco-labels are created equal. Some certification programs are highly respected and rigorously monitored, while others are more dubious or even created by companies themselves as a marketing tool. Be sure to look for well-established, credible certifications such as:

- **Fair Trade**: Ensures ethical sourcing and support for workers in developing countries.

- **Energy Star**: Indicates energy-efficient products.
- **Forest Stewardship Council (FSC)**: Identifies products made from responsibly sourced wood.
- **USDA Organic**: Certifies that food products are produced without synthetic chemicals or GMOs.

However, some companies may create their own "green" labels or use certifications that aren't verified by independent third parties. For instance, the term "eco-certified" or "green seal" may not have any standard or criteria behind it. Be cautious of vague or unclear labels that don't provide specific information about their certification process.

3. Investigate the Entire Lifecycle of the Product

To assess whether a product is truly sustainable, it's important to consider its entire lifecycle—from production to consumption to disposal. Some companies may promote one environmentally friendly feature (such as using recycled materials in packaging) while ignoring the overall impact of the product's lifecycle. For example, a company may advertise an eco-friendly detergent but fail to address the unsustainable practices involved in sourcing the raw materials or manufacturing the product.

In particular, consumers should consider:

- **Material sourcing**: Where are the raw materials coming from? Are they sustainably harvested or extracted?
- **Production processes**: How energy- and resource-intensive is the manufacturing process? Are toxic chemicals used in production?
- **Transportation and shipping**: How far has the product traveled to get to the consumer? Long supply chains often contribute to significant carbon footprints.
- **End-of-life**: Is the product recyclable, biodegradable, or compostable? Will it contribute to landfill waste after use?

4. Check for Transparency and Specificity

A key sign of greenwashing is a lack of transparency. Companies that are genuinely committed to sustainability are usually eager to share details about their practices, including the sourcing of raw materials, the sustainability of their supply chains, and how they're measuring their environmental impact. Be wary of companies that are vague or evasive when asked about their environmental practices. If a brand refuses to provide specific information or details on how it's achieving its sustainability goals, it's likely a red flag.

Transparency extends to third-party audits and external certifications as well. Companies committed to sustainability often subject themselves to independent verification to prove their claims. Look for annual sustainability reports, third-party audits, or certifications from reputable organizations that demonstrate accountability.

5. Follow the Money: Corporate Track Record

One of the best ways to evaluate a company's environmental claims is to look at its overall track record. Is the company's history consistent with its "green" claims, or does it have a history of environmental violations, poor labor practices, or significant contributions to pollution? Many corporations that engage in greenwashing are only superficially concerned with sustainability, as their long-term business model and operations are still based on environmental degradation.

For example, many oil and gas companies continue to promote "green" initiatives such as renewable energy investments while still investing heavily in fossil fuel exploration and contributing to major environmental damage. Investigating whether the company has publicly lobbied against stronger climate regulations or environmental protections is also a helpful indicator. Companies involved in greenwashing often use their "green" marketing as a distraction from their overall harmful impact.

6. Utilize Consumer Resources and Apps

There are numerous resources available to help consumers make more informed, eco-conscious purchasing decisions. Tools like **Good On You** for fashion, **Ecolabel Index,** and **Earth Hero** offer rankings and reviews on sustainability practices for a wide range of products and companies. Apps like **Buycott** and **HowGood** allow consumers to scan barcodes and access a product's environmental and ethical credentials, making it easier to identify products that align with personal values.

In addition, many sustainability advocacy groups and watchdog organizations, like **Greenpeace** and the **Environmental Working Group**, conduct regular investigations and release reports about corporate greenwashing, helping consumers stay informed about which companies are genuinely eco-friendly and which are not.

Greenwashing is a major obstacle to the global movement for sustainability. By using deceptive marketing tactics, corporations have the ability to distract consumers from the real environmental changes that are needed to combat climate change, deforestation, pollution, and other crises. But as consumers, we have the power to fight back. By learning to identify greenwashing, questioning ambiguous claims, and holding companies accountable for their actions, we can demand real, verifiable environmental change.

The key to making a difference lies in awareness—understanding how companies use greenwashing to manipulate consumer behavior and arming ourselves with the tools and knowledge to make informed decisions. When consumers prioritize transparency and accountability, they send a strong message to corporations that true sustainability isn't just a marketing strategy, but a necessity for our planet's future.

The real challenge, however, goes beyond individual consumer choices. To create the systemic change necessary for a sustainable world, we need to demand stronger regulations, more robust certifications, and greater corporate accountability. But by starting with informed, ethical purchasing decisions, we can begin to shift the tide away from greenwashing toward a more genuine commitment to a sustainable, just, and environmentally conscious future.

The power to combat greenwashing lies within the hands of consumers, who can use their purchasing power to hold corporations accountable for their environmental impact. By learning how to identify greenwashing, supporting companies with a proven commitment to sustainability, and demanding greater transparency from businesses, consumers can play a crucial role in driving real, meaningful change. Ultimately, the fight against greenwashing is part of the broader movement for environmental justice, and every informed choice we make contributes to a more sustainable, transparent, and accountable global economy.

Chapter 4

Sustainable Solutions
What's Working, What's Not

As the world grapples with the growing environmental crises of climate change, biodiversity loss, pollution, and resource depletion, the call for solutions has never been more urgent. A wide range of approaches have been proposed and implemented at local, national, and global levels, from cutting-edge technologies to policy initiatives aimed at reducing our ecological footprint. While some solutions show promise, many are fraught with limitations that prevent them from being the panacea we need. This section takes a critical look at the most commonly discussed solutions to the environmental crisis, exploring what is working, what isn't, and why even well-intentioned efforts may fall short.

1. Renewable Energy: Transitioning from Fossil Fuels

There is broad consensus that renewable energy—including solar, wind, hydro, and geothermal—must replace fossil fuels in order to reduce greenhouse gas emissions and mitigate the impacts of climate change. As countries around the world accelerate their transition to cleaner energy sources, renewable energy has seen significant growth. In 2022, for example, renewable energy accounted for nearly 30% of the global energy mix, with solar and wind leading the charge.

Solar power has become one of the most widely adopted clean energy solutions. The price of solar panels has dropped dramatically in the last decade, making solar energy more accessible to both homeowners and businesses. Similarly, wind energy, particularly offshore wind, has made considerable strides, with countries like Denmark, China, and the United Kingdom investing heavily in wind farms.

However, despite the rapid growth of renewables, there are significant limitations that hinder their full potential. The most pressing issue is energy storage. Solar and wind energy are intermittent—solar energy is only generated when the sun is shining, and wind energy depends on wind speeds. As a result, we need robust and affordable energy storage technologies to ensure a stable and reliable energy supply. Currently, batteries such as **lithium-ion batteries** are commonly used to store energy, but they have their own set of problems: **limited lifespan, high costs, and environmental concerns** about mining for the raw materials required, such as lithium and cobalt.

Additionally, the infrastructure needed to integrate renewable energy into the existing grid is still underdeveloped in many regions. In countries like the United States, where the power grid is aging and fragmented, upgrading and modernizing the infrastructure to accommodate renewables is a complex and expensive task. Without these upgrades, the potential of renewable energy is stunted.

Furthermore, while solar and wind are cleaner alternatives to fossil fuels, they are not entirely free of environmental impact. For example, the production of solar panels and wind turbines involves the extraction of minerals and metals, such as rare earth elements and silicon, which can have environmental consequences, including habitat destruction and pollution from mining processes. While the long-term environmental benefits outweigh these impacts, the ecological cost of scaling renewable energy systems still requires careful consideration and improvement.

2. Electric Vehicles (EVs): A Cleaner Transportation Future?

The push for electric vehicles (EVs) has been one of the most visible and discussed aspects of the transition to a more sustainable world. EVs offer a promising solution to the transportation sector, which is responsible for a significant share of global greenhouse gas emissions. In 2021, electric car sales worldwide grew by 108%, with an increasing number of countries announcing plans to phase out gasoline and diesel cars in favor of electric alternatives. Major car manufacturers, including Tesla, GM, and Volkswagen, are now investing billions into EV production, while governments are offering subsidies and incentives to accelerate adoption.

EVs are indeed a cleaner alternative to conventional gasoline or diesel-powered vehicles. They produce zero tailpipe emissions, which significantly reduce air pollution, particularly in urban areas. When powered by renewable energy sources, EVs can effectively reduce the carbon footprint of transportation.

However, there are **several limitations** to the widespread adoption of electric vehicles. First and foremost is the issue of **battery production and disposal**. While EVs themselves are clean, the manufacturing of lithium-ion batteries used in EVs requires the extraction of minerals like lithium, cobalt, and nickel—a process that can be ecologically harmful, involving **habitat destruction, water contamination, and human rights abuses** in some regions where mining is concentrated. The environmental impact of battery production is particularly concerning given that EV adoption is increasing at a rapid pace, which will likely increase demand for these minerals.

Moreover, while battery technology is improving, many of the batteries currently in use have limited recyclability and can create environmental problems when disposed of improperly. Although recycling technologies for EV batteries are being developed, they are not yet widespread or efficient enough to mitigate the growing waste problem associated with used batteries.

Another barrier is charging infrastructure. While EVs have made significant inroads in urban areas, rural regions often lack sufficient charging stations, making long-distance travel difficult for many drivers. Additionally, the production of the electricity required to charge EVs can still come from fossil fuels, which negates some of the environmental benefits of switching to electric vehicles.

Finally, there are concerns about the overall carbon footprint of EVs when considering their entire lifecycle, including production, operation, and disposal. While driving an EV is cleaner than a traditional car, the initial environmental cost of manufacturing an EV (particularly the battery) is higher than that of a conventional vehicle. If the electricity used to charge EVs comes from non-renewable sources, the environmental benefits are further diminished.

3. Carbon Capture and Storage (CCS): A Hopeful but Unproven Solution

Carbon capture and storage (CCS) has been hailed as one of the most promising technological solutions to combat climate change. The idea behind CCS is simple: capture carbon dioxide (CO_2) emissions from industrial sources (such as power plants and factories) before they can enter the atmosphere, and then store it underground in geological formations or use it in other processes, such as enhanced oil recovery.

Proponents argue that CCS could play a critical role in reducing global CO_2 emissions, particularly for industries that are difficult to decarbonize, such as cement and steel manufacturing. Some even argue that CCS could allow for the continued use of fossil fuels while mitigating their impact on the climate.

However, the reality of scaling CCS to the level necessary to make a meaningful impact on global emissions is still uncertain. The technology remains expensive, with high operational and maintenance costs. Additionally, the storage of CO_2 underground raises concerns about leakage, with potential environmental consequences if CO_2 were to escape from storage sites. There have also been several high-profile failures of CCS projects, including the Kemper County plant in Mississippi, which was abandoned after failing to meet its performance goals and running vastly over budget.

Currently, only a few commercial CCS projects exist, and they are mostly small-scale. For CCS to make a significant difference, it would need to be deployed at a much larger scale—something that is technically, economically, and politically challenging. Moreover, relying on CCS could delay the much-needed transition away from fossil fuels, allowing industries to continue emitting CO_2 while relying on unproven technology as a safety net.

4. Plant-Based Diets and Sustainable Agriculture: A Step in the Right Direction

The environmental impact of our food choices is immense, and one solution gaining traction is the move toward plant-based diets and sustainable agriculture. The meat and dairy industries are among the largest contributors to greenhouse gas emissions, deforestation, and water usage. Shifting to plant-based foods, along with improving agricultural practices, can significantly reduce the environmental footprint of our food system.

Plant-based food companies, such as **Beyond Meat and Impossible Foods**, have risen to prominence by offering plant-based alternatives to traditional meat products. These companies claim that by replacing animal products with plant-based options, we can reduce carbon emissions, water use, and land degradation. And indeed, studies show that the carbon footprint of plant-based foods is generally lower than that of animal-based foods, particularly when comparing beef and pork to plant-based substitutes.

However, there are several limitations to this approach. For one, the production of plant-based foods is not without environmental consequences. Crops like soy, almonds, and avocados, while plant-based, can also have significant ecological impacts. For example, large-scale soy production, often linked to deforestation in the Amazon, is a major driver of biodiversity loss and habitat destruction.

Moreover, the push for plant-based diets often ignores the environmental impact of monoculture farming practices, where vast areas of land are dedicated to growing a single crop. This approach depletes soil nutrients, harms biodiversity, and can increase reliance on chemical pesticides and fertilizers. To truly create a sustainable food system, we need a shift toward regenerative agriculture, which emphasizes soil health, biodiversity, and reduced chemical inputs.

The solutions we have at our disposal to tackle the environmental crisis are varied and, in many cases, promising. Renewable energy technologies, electric vehicles, carbon capture, and plant-based diets all offer tangible benefits that can contribute to reducing our global ecological footprint. However, none of these solutions are without limitations. Whether it's the environmental impact of manufacturing batteries for EVs, the logistical challenges of scaling renewable energy infrastructure, or the ethical dilemmas associated with large-scale agricultural practices, each solution presents its own set of hurdles.

To ensure that these solutions move us closer to a sustainable future, we must look beyond the technological fixes alone. We need to address the underlying causes of environmental degradation—overconsumption, unsustainable business models, and inadequate policies—and ensure that solutions are implemented in a holistic and responsible way.

Alternative Solutions Showing Promise

While many of the current solutions to the environmental crisis have limitations, there are alternative approaches and emerging technologies that show real promise. These solutions, though less mainstream or still in early stages of development, have the potential to radically transform how we produce, consume, and interact with the natural world. From regenerative agriculture to innovative building materials and bio-based solutions, these alternatives could be the key to creating a more sustainable, resilient future for our planet.

1. Regenerative Agriculture: Revitalizing the Soil

Regenerative agriculture has emerged as one of the most exciting alternatives to conventional industrial farming practices, which often rely on harmful chemicals, monoculture planting, and resource-intensive methods. Regenerative practices focus on rebuilding soil health, increasing biodiversity, and reducing carbon emissions by working in harmony with nature rather than exploiting it. Unlike conventional agriculture, which often depletes the soil, regenerative methods enrich the soil by incorporating practices like cover cropping, no-till farming, crop rotation, and composting.

One of the most significant benefits of regenerative agriculture is its ability to act as a carbon sink. Soil, when managed correctly, has the potential to sequester large amounts of carbon dioxide, helping mitigate climate change. According to the Rodale Institute, transitioning 12% of the world's agricultural land to regenerative practices could draw down 100% of current annual global CO_2 emissions. By rebuilding soil organic matter, regenerative farming increases the soil's ability to store water and nutrients, improving food security and resilience to droughts and floods.

Real-world examples of regenerative agriculture are already proving its effectiveness. In the U.S., **The Savory Institute** is leading the way in promoting holistic grazing techniques that mimic the natural patterns of grazing animals. This approach has been shown to restore degraded grasslands, increase biodiversity, and improve soil health. Additionally, regenerative farming has been successfully implemented by farmers across the globe, from Australia's Outback to the U.K., where farmers are growing diverse crops and practicing agroforestry to restore ecosystems while maintaining productivity.

However, while regenerative agriculture shows great promise, it's still far from being universally adopted. A key challenge is the transition from industrial farming methods to regenerative practices, which can require significant upfront investment, time, and education. Moreover, there is a need for policy support and government incentives to help farmers make this shift, as well as a market that values the environmental benefits of regenerative agriculture.

2. Circular Economy: Redefining Waste and Resources

A circular economy is a radically different model from the traditional "take-make-dispose" linear economy. In a circular economy, the focus is on resource efficiency, waste reduction, and product life extension. The goal is to create a system where resources are kept in use for as long as possible, products are reused and repaired, and waste is minimized or eliminated entirely.

In the context of environmental sustainability, the circular economy has immense potential to address issues like plastic pollution, resource depletion, and overconsumption. Instead of relying on virgin materials, a circular economy encourages businesses to use recycled materials, design products for durability, and create systems for reuse and remanufacturing. For example, Apple has implemented a recycling program where old iPhones are disassembled by robots, and their valuable components, such as rare earth metals and precious metals, are recovered and reused. Similarly, Patagonia has long been a pioneer in creating products that are designed to be repaired, recycled, or reused, reducing waste in the fashion industry.

One of the most exciting developments within the circular economy is the concept of a zero-waste society. Cities like Kamigamo, Japan and Capannori, Italy have implemented comprehensive zero-waste policies that focus on reducing the consumption of single-use plastics, composting organic waste, and diverting materials from landfills. These approaches not only reduce waste but also create local jobs in recycling, repair, and remanufacturing industries, contributing to economic resilience and creating a more sustainable society.

The challenge in scaling the circular economy lies in changing business models and consumer behavior. Many businesses still prioritize short-term profits over long-term sustainability, making it difficult to transition to circular models. Moreover, consumers are accustomed to a linear system of consumption, which often involves buying new products and discarding the old ones. Shifting to a circular economy requires significant changes in both corporate practices and consumer culture, along with strong policies and incentives from governments.

3. Biomimicry: Learning from Nature

Biomimicry is an approach that looks to nature for inspiration in solving human problems, particularly in the design of sustainable products, systems, and processes. Nature has evolved solutions to challenges like energy efficiency, waste recycling, and sustainable building materials over billions of years. By observing and mimicking natural processes, humans can create more sustainable technologies that align with the planet's ecological systems.

One of the most famous examples of biomimicry is the design of **The Eastgate Centre** in Zimbabwe, a building that mimics the termite mounds in the region to maintain a stable internal temperature. Termites are known for their ability to regulate the temperature inside their mounds, despite the extreme heat outside. Engineers applied this principle to design a building that uses natural ventilation and minimizes the need for air conditioning, resulting in significant energy savings.

In the realm of materials science, biodegradable plastics made from plant fibers and algae are another example of biomimicry. Companies like Ecovative Design are developing materials that imitate the structure of natural fibers, using them to create compostable products that reduce our reliance on petrochemical-based plastics. Additionally, the development of self-healing materials, which mimic the ability of natural systems to repair themselves, could revolutionize industries like construction, transportation, and electronics, reducing waste and extending the lifespan of products.

However, despite the promise of biomimicry, there are challenges in scaling these solutions. Nature-inspired designs often require more time and research to implement, and they may face resistance due to the higher upfront costs compared to conventional technologies. Additionally, while biomimicry can offer sustainable solutions, it is still important to consider the full life cycle impact of these innovations, including their resource use, manufacturing processes, and disposal.

4. Alternative Building Materials: Sustainable Construction for a Growing Population

As urbanization continues at an unprecedented rate, the demand for sustainable building materials has grown. Traditional construction methods, such as concrete and steel, are resource-intensive and contribute significantly to carbon emissions. In response, a number of alternative materials are being explored that are both sustainable and scalable.

One such material is hempcrete, a concrete-like material made from the fibers of the hemp plant. **Hempcrete** is lightweight, highly insulating, and carbon-negative—meaning it sequesters more carbon than is released during its production. Additionally, hemp can be grown quickly and with relatively low environmental impact, making it an ideal crop for sustainable building. Hemp houses are already being built in places like Europe and North America, showing the potential of this material to reduce the environmental footprint of construction.

Another alternative material is **mycelium**—the root structure of fungi, which can be used to create biodegradable bricksand insulation. Mycelium-based materials are lightweight, versatile, and can be produced with minimal energy. Companies like **Ecovative** Design are already creating products from mycelium that are used in packaging, furniture, and construction, demonstrating the potential of fungi as a sustainable material source.

Recycled materials, such as recycled plastic, wood, and glass, are also increasingly being used in construction, reducing the need for virgin materials and diverting waste from landfills. For example, the Plastic Road project in the Netherlands is experimenting with recycled plastic bricks that can be used for building roads, which offer durability and reduce waste.

However, while these alternative materials show great promise, their widespread adoption faces challenges. These materials often need further research and development to ensure they are as durable and cost-effective as traditional construction materials. Scaling production and developing supply chains for alternative building materials also requires significant investment and infrastructure development.

Regenerative agriculture, circular economies, biomimicry, and alternative building materials offer exciting possibilities for a sustainable future. These approaches are rooted in principles that prioritize the long-term health of ecosystems, the efficient use of resources, and a commitment to circularity. While they are not without challenges, they represent a radical departure from the current trajectory of environmental degradation.

As these solutions evolve, they have the potential to reshape industries, create new economic opportunities, and mitigate the worst impacts of climate change. However, their widespread adoption will require innovation, collaboration, and a shift in both consumer behavior and corporate priorities. Ultimately, these alternative solutions could play a key role in the broader transition toward a sustainable world, where human activities and the planet's ecological systems can thrive in harmony.

A Critical Assessment of What's Truly Effective

As we look to a sustainable future, it is essential to critically evaluate which of the proposed solutions are genuinely effective in addressing the environmental crises we face, and which may simply be short-term fixes or half-measures. While solutions such as renewable energy, electric vehicles, and regenerative agriculture offer great promise, their current impact often falls short of what is necessary to meet the scale of the challenges ahead. We need to move beyond optimistic projections and ask whether these technologies and practices can deliver what they promise—and if not, how we can improve them to make a real, lasting difference.

1. Renewable Energy: The Race to Decarbonize

Renewable energy, particularly solar and wind, is widely regarded as the key to reducing global dependence on fossil fuels. While these technologies have made impressive strides in terms of cost reductions and adoption, their ability to decarbonize the global economy remains limited by several factors. First, renewable energy sources like solar and wind remain highly dependent on intermittency—the fact that they only generate power when the sun shines or the wind blows. As a result, the global transition to renewables requires a massive expansion of energy storage technologies, but solutions such as batteries and hydrogen storage are still in early stages of development, with cost and efficiency barriers preventing them from being viable at scale.

Moreover, the mining of critical minerals needed for renewable technologies—such as lithium, cobalt, and rare earth metals—poses its own set of environmental challenges. While these technologies are certainly cleaner than fossil fuels, the environmental impact of sourcing and refining these materials must not be overlooked. The clean energy transition is therefore not as straightforward as it may seem; it requires a careful balancing act between reducing emissions from energy production and minimizing the environmental cost of producing renewable technologies.

The promise of renewable energy has yet to be fully realized, particularly in developing countries where energy access is still limited. Without substantial investment in energy infrastructure and storage technologies, renewables alone cannot meet the global demand for consistent, reliable energy. This makes it clear that renewable energy is a vital piece of the puzzle, but it must be part of a broader, more integrated approach to achieving sustainability.

2. Electric Vehicles: Shifting Transportation Toward Clean Energy

Electric vehicles (EVs) have been heralded as one of the most important tools for reducing emissions from the transportation sector. EVs are often seen as a cleaner alternative to gasoline and diesel cars, and their popularity has skyrocketed in recent years. However, a critical assessment of EVs reveals that while they have some environmental benefits, they are not a perfect solution.

At the core of the issue is battery production. As mentioned earlier, lithium-ion batteries, which power most EVs, require the extraction of minerals that often come with significant environmental and ethical costs. The mining of lithium in places like the Atacama Desert in Chile and Cobalt in the Democratic Republic of the Congo often involves harmful practices, such as water depletion, pollution, and human rights violations. These issues must be addressed if the global EV market is to scale sustainably.

Additionally, while EVs do produce zero tailpipe emissions, their carbon footprint over the course of their entire life cycle—considering manufacturing, battery production, and eventual disposal—can still be higher than conventional vehicles, especially when the electricity used to charge them comes from fossil fuel-based sources. The success of EVs as a climate solution, therefore, depends largely on the success of transitioning to renewable energy grids.

EVs also do little to address the broader issue of overconsumption and urban sprawl. The environmental impact of automobile culture—from congestion and air pollution to the vast amount of resources required to build and maintain roads and infrastructure—remains a significant concern. Shifting away from car dependency through public transit, cycling infrastructure, and urban planning is a critical complement to the rise of EVs.

While electric vehicles are a step in the right direction, their potential for achieving meaningful environmental change depends on addressing both the full life cycle of their production and the societal context in which they are deployed. In isolation, they are not the magic bullet for reducing our transportation sector's emissions.

3. Regenerative Agriculture: Can It Scale?

Regenerative agriculture is one of the most promising solutions for restoring ecosystems, sequestering carbon, and promoting food security. By rebuilding soil health, regenerating biodiversity, and reducing reliance on harmful pesticides and fertilizers, regenerative farming offers an environmentally friendly alternative to industrial agriculture. Practices like no-till farming, cover cropping, and rotational grazing can help reverse the degradation caused by industrial practices, allowing for more resilient and productive farms.

Yet, while regenerative agriculture has been shown to deliver strong results in certain contexts, it also faces significant hurdles when it comes to scaling. First, the adoption of regenerative practices requires farmers to shift from conventional methods to new ways of farming, which often entails initial costs and risk—especially when market incentives are skewed toward conventional monoculture crops. Despite the growing interest in regenerative agriculture, policies and subsidies still largely favor industrial farming, which can make the transition financially challenging for many farmers.

Furthermore, regenerative practices require a deep understanding of local ecosystems, making widespread training and support essential for ensuring success. Unlike conventional farming, which relies heavily on industrial inputs, regenerative farming demands a more nuanced and knowledge-intensive approach. This makes it difficult for large-scale, industrial players to adopt these practices without a complete overhaul of farming models and a rethinking of global food systems.

Finally, regenerative agriculture can make a significant contribution to carbon sequestration but is unlikely to offset the full extent of global emissions on its own. While it can play an important role in creating more sustainable food systems, it is not a silver bullet. Complementary solutions, such as sustainable forestry, alternative proteins, and policy reforms aimed at reducing food waste, will need to work in tandem with regenerative agriculture for it to have a substantial, long-term impact on climate change.

4. The Circular Economy: Redefining Consumption

The circular economy represents a transformative shift away from the traditional linear model of production, consumption, and disposal. By focusing on resource efficiency, product durability, and waste reduction, a circular economy could revolutionize industries ranging from fashion to electronics to construction. Recycling, remanufacturing, and upcycling are all central tenets of a circular approach, ensuring that products are reused, repaired, or recycled rather than discarded.

However, the transition to a circular economy is fraught with challenges. First and foremost, it requires a fundamental shift in how industries design and produce goods. Products must be designed with their entire life cycle in mind, which includes ensuring that they can be easily disassembled, repaired, or recycled. Currently, many products are designed with planned obsolescence in mind, making it difficult to incorporate circular principles without a massive overhaul of production systems.

Second, for a circular economy to truly work at scale, it requires massive investments in recycling infrastructure and waste management systems. While some regions, such as parts of Europe, have made strides in this area, many countries, particularly in the Global South, lack the resources or infrastructure to properly recycle materials, meaning valuable materials often end up in landfills or the ocean.

The circular economy also faces cultural barriers. Consumerism remains deeply ingrained in many societies, and the desire for new, cheap products often trumps the need for sustainability. Until there is a major shift in both consumer behavior and corporate priorities, the potential for the circular economy to become the dominant model will remain limited.

The solutions we have at our disposal are indeed diverse and varied, from renewable energy and electric vehicles to regenerative agriculture and the circular economy. Each holds promise, but each also has its limitations and challenges that must be critically addressed if they are to be effective in the fight against climate change and environmental degradation. While renewable energy and EVs have made significant strides, their scalability and the environmental impact of their production remain concerns. Regenerative agriculture offers a much-needed alternative to industrial farming but needs broader adoption and support. The circular economy promises a more sustainable model of consumption but faces substantial barriers in infrastructure, behavior, and business models.

In the face of these challenges, it is clear that no single solution will suffice. Instead, a combination of approaches is required, one that integrates technological innovation, sustainable practices, and systemic change. Policymakers, businesses, and individuals alike must recognize that achieving sustainability is a complex, multifaceted task, and one that demands not only the adoption of new technologies but also a radical shift in how we produce, consume, and live. Only by working together to create a more holistic, interconnected approach to sustainability can we hope to rise to the challenges that lie ahead.

Chapter 5

The Role of Sustainable Agriculture in the Future

As the world faces a growing array of environmental crises—climate change, biodiversity loss, and the degradation of ecosystems—few sectors are as pivotal in both causing and addressing these issues as agriculture. The way we produce food, the land management practices we use, and the policies that shape our food systems are inextricably linked to the planet's health. Yet, the conventional methods of industrial agriculture—those built on monoculture, excessive chemical inputs, and resource-intensive practices—are among the largest contributors to environmental degradation.

If we are to have any hope of addressing the intertwined challenges of climate change, food security, and soil degradation, we must look to fundamentally reshape the way we farm and manage our land. Sustainable agriculture represents a critical shift away from the harmful practices of the industrial farming model toward a system that works in harmony with the planet's ecosystems and preserves natural resources for future generations.

The need for this transformation has never been more urgent. By some estimates, one-third of the world's soils are already degraded, and climate change is expected to exacerbate these problems, threatening agricultural productivity in many regions. Meanwhile, global food demand continues to rise, driven by a growing population and shifting dietary patterns. According to the United Nations, the world will need to produce 70% more food by 2050 to meet the needs of a population that is expected to exceed 9 billion people. To meet this demand while ensuring the health of the planet and the well-being of future generations, we must not only change how we grow food but also rethink the very systems that govern our agricultural practices.

The Impact of Industrial Agriculture

To understand the necessity of a global shift to sustainable farming, it is essential to look at the environmental toll of industrial agriculture. The conventional farming model, which has dominated the global food system since the mid-20th century, is characterized by large-scale monocultures, extensive use of chemical pesticides and fertilizers, and heavy reliance on fossil fuels for machinery and transportation.

- **Soil degradation** is perhaps the most visible consequence of industrial farming. The widespread use of chemical fertilizers and pesticides, combined with the depletion of organic matter through monocropping, has led to soil erosion, nutrient depletion, and the loss of microbial diversity. According to the UN Food and Agriculture Organization (FAO), the world's soils are being eroded at a rate

10 to 40 times faster than they are being replenished, with serious implications for food production and ecosystem health.

- **Water scarcity** is another growing issue. Industrial agriculture accounts for around 70% of global freshwater use, and in many regions, irrigation practices have led to the depletion of aquifers and the pollution of water supplies through runoff of synthetic fertilizers and pesticides. This overuse of water is unsustainable, especially in areas already facing drought or declining freshwater resources.

- **Greenhouse gas emissions** from industrial agriculture are also a major contributor to climate change. The production, transportation, and processing of agricultural products—particularly in livestock farming—are responsible for around 24% of global greenhouse gas emissions. This includes methane emissions from livestock, nitrous oxide from fertilizers, and carbon dioxide from land-use changes, such as deforestation for agriculture.

- **Biodiversity loss** is yet another critical concern. The extensive use of pesticides and herbicides, the draining of wetlands, and the destruction of forests to make way for agricultural land have all contributed to the loss of wildlife habitats and the extinction of species. In many parts of the world, industrial farming has replaced diverse ecosystems with sterile monocultures, further diminishing biodiversity and ecosystem resilience.

Given the scale of these challenges, it is clear that the industrial agriculture model is not only environmentally unsustainable but also increasingly incompatible with the needs of a growing global population. To ensure food security, environmental sustainability, and economic stability, a comprehensive transformation toward sustainable agriculture is not just desirable—it is imperative.

Why a Shift to Sustainable Farming Is Essential

Sustainable agriculture, at its core, is about working with nature, not against it. It seeks to maintain the health of the soil, water, air, and biodiversity, while also producing food in a way that is economically viable and socially just. This means moving away from practices that degrade natural resources and toward methods that enhance environmental health, protect ecosystems, and promote resilience to climate change.

Some of the primary reasons why a shift to sustainable farming is essential include:

- **Soil Health and Carbon Sequestration**: One of the most compelling reasons for shifting to sustainable farming is the ability of certain farming practices to improve soil health and sequester carbon. Practices like no-till farming, cover cropping, and rotational grazing improve soil structure, enhance organic matter, and reduce erosion, making the land more resilient to extreme weather events.

Furthermore, healthy soils act as a carbon sink, pulling CO2 from the atmosphere and storing it in the soil. In fact, if regenerative agricultural practices were adopted on a global scale, it could play a significant role in mitigating climate change by pulling large amounts of carbon from the air. According to the **Rodale Institute**, transitioning just 12% of global cropland to regenerative agriculture could draw down enough carbon to offset all global emissions from fossil fuels.

- **Biodiversity Restoration**: Sustainable farming practices can also help restore biodiversity, both in agricultural systems and surrounding ecosystems. By diversifying crops and integrating agroforestry and permaculture techniques, farmers can create environments that support a variety of plant and animal species, helping to prevent species extinction and support healthier ecosystems. Integrating wildlife corridors into farm landscapes and reducing the use of toxic chemicals can enhance biodiversity while improving overall farm productivity.

- **Water Conservation**: Practices like drip irrigation, rainwater harvesting, and conservation tillage can significantly reduce water consumption and improve water-use efficiency in farming. Sustainable agriculture also reduces water pollution caused by runoff from synthetic fertilizers and pesticides, which often end up in local rivers, lakes, and groundwater, degrading water quality and harming aquatic life. By adopting systems that conserve water and reduce pollution, sustainable farming not only helps to protect our vital freshwater resources but also makes agriculture more resilient to droughts and water scarcity.

- **Local Food Security and Resilience**: Sustainable farming is inherently more local and diverse than industrial agriculture. By supporting small-scale farmers and focusing on regional food systems, we can build more resilient food systems that are better able to withstand shocks such as climate disasters, pandemics, or supply chain disruptions. A shift toward more local and seasonal food production can also reduce the carbon footprint associated with food transportation, further contributing to emissions reductions.

- **Economic Viability**: Sustainable farming has the potential to offer long-term economic benefits for farmers. While it may require an upfront investment in transitioning to new practices, over time, sustainable farming methods tend to be more cost-effective because they reduce the need for expensive chemical inputs and machinery. Moreover, sustainable practices can improve yields over time by building healthy soils and creating more resilient farming systems that are less reliant on external inputs. Farmers who adopt regenerative practices often report improved profitability, as healthier soils lead to increased crop productivity and reduced susceptibility to pests and diseases.

The need for a global shift toward sustainable farming is clear. The environmental, economic, and social challenges posed by industrial agriculture are too great to ignore, and the consequences of inaction will be felt for generations to come. Sustainable farming offers a path forward—one that aligns food production with environmental stewardship, fosters greater resilience to climate change, and promotes a healthier, more equitable food system for all.

However, the transition will not be easy. It requires the commitment of governments, businesses, and consumers, as well as a concerted effort to scale up successful models of sustainable agriculture worldwide. By investing in sustainable farming practices, we have an opportunity to heal the planet, ensure food security for future generations, and create a more just and resilient global food system.

Examples of Sustainable Agriculture Models

While the need for a global shift toward sustainable farming is urgent, it is equally important to recognize that sustainable agricultural practices are not theoretical or distant goals—they are already being implemented successfully across the world. From small-scale community initiatives to large-scale regenerative farms, there are numerous examples of farming systems that are both environmentally viable and economically sustainable. These models demonstrate that sustainable agriculture is not only possible but can be an essential part of the future of food production.

In this section, we will explore several notable examples of sustainable agriculture models that offer practical solutions to many of the issues faced by industrial farming. These examples show how sustainable practices can work in diverse contexts, from temperate climates to arid regions, and can be applied to a wide range of crops, livestock, and farming systems.

1. Regenerative Agriculture: Revitalizing the Land

Regenerative agriculture goes beyond sustainability by seeking to restore and enhance the health of ecosystems. Rather than simply minimizing harm, regenerative practices aim to regenerate and improve soil fertility, biodiversity, and water retention. Regenerative farmers focus on practices that rebuild rather than deplete natural resources.

Key principles of regenerative agriculture include:

- **No-till farming:** This involves planting crops without disturbing the soil through plowing. No-till farming helps to preserve soil structure, prevent erosion, and encourage the growth of soil microbes that are essential for soil health.
- **Cover cropping:** Planting specific crops, such as legumes or grasses, during the off-season helps protect the soil from erosion, improve soil fertility, and promote biodiversity. These crops also help sequester carbon and fix nitrogen in the soil.
- **Rotational grazing:** This practice involves moving livestock between different pastures to prevent overgrazing and allow grasslands to regenerate. It mimics natural grazing patterns, increasing soil health and promoting plant growth.

Real-World Example: The Rodale Institute in the U.S.

The Rodale Institute, based in Pennsylvania, is one of the leading advocates and practitioners of regenerative farming. Their long-term studies demonstrate that regenerative practices can significantly improve soil health, increase biodiversity, and even sequester carbon. The institute's research shows that regenerative methods can yield comparable, if not superior, crop production compared to conventional industrial farming, all while improving the land's ability to store carbon.

The Rodale Institute's Regenerative Organic Certification program is a growing movement that certifies farms and products that meet high standards of environmental and social sustainability. The Institute's research has proven that, with the right management techniques, farming can regenerate the land while reducing greenhouse gas emissions—fighting climate change while feeding people.

2. Agroforestry: Integrating Trees and Crops

Agroforestry is a practice that integrates trees, shrubs, and other vegetation into agricultural landscapes. It combines the benefits of forestry with traditional crop and livestock farming, creating a more diversified, resilient farming system. Agroforestry systems can provide multiple sources of income, restore ecosystems, and enhance biodiversity.

Key benefits of agroforestry include:

- **Carbon sequestration:** Trees naturally capture carbon dioxide from the atmosphere and store it in their biomass and the surrounding soil. Agroforestry systems are highly effective at sequestering carbon and improving the farm's climate resilience.
- **Biodiversity enhancement:** By adding trees and shrubs to agricultural land, agroforestry systems create habitats for wildlife, increasing biodiversity and promoting ecosystem services such as pest control and pollination.
- **Water management:** Tree roots help to stabilize soil and prevent erosion, while the canopy provides shade and reduces water evaporation from the soil. This is especially important in areas prone to drought.

Real-World Example: The International Centre for Research in Agroforestry (ICRAF)

The International Centre for Research in Agroforestry (ICRAF) has been at the forefront of developing and promoting agroforestry techniques around the world. In Kenya, ICRAF's research has shown that **integrating Moringa and Acacia trees with maize and bean crops** can increase yields by up to 50% while providing additional sources of income through timber and tree products. These agroforestry systems help restore degraded soils, improve water retention, and reduce the need for chemical fertilizers.

Agroforestry is particularly beneficial in regions experiencing land degradation or desertification, where it helps to restore soil fertility and water retention, making the land more resilient to climate impacts.

3. Permaculture: Designing Sustainable, Closed-Loop Systems

Permaculture is a holistic approach to farming that emphasizes the creation of self-sustaining, closed-loop systems where waste is minimized, and resources are recycled. The goal of permaculture is to design agricultural systems that mimic natural ecosystems, creating harmony between human activity and nature. Unlike traditional agriculture, permaculture designs take into account energy flow, biodiversity, and soil health, creating a system where all elements work together synergistically.

Key principles of permaculture include:

- **Diversity:** Permaculture systems focus on growing a wide variety of plants and animals to create a more resilient and balanced ecosystem. Polyculture (growing many types of crops together) replaces monoculture, which reduces the risk of pests and disease while promoting biodiversity.
- **Water conservation:** By using methods like rainwater harvesting, swales, and mulching, permaculture systems capture and manage water more effectively, reducing the need for irrigation and minimizing water wastage.
- **Waste recycling:** In permaculture, waste is viewed as a resource. Organic waste is composted and returned to the soil, while livestock manure is used as fertilizer. This closed-loop system reduces the need for external inputs and minimizes pollution.

Real-World Example: The Djan-Djan Permaculture Project in Haiti

The Djan-Djan Permaculture Project, led by the Haitian Permaculture Initiative, is an excellent example of permaculture practices being used to combat deforestation, soil erosion, and poverty in Haiti. The project focuses on training local farmers to use permaculture techniques to restore degraded land and improve food security. Through practices like contour planting, rainwater harvesting, and the creation of food forests, the project has helped to restore ecosystems, improve crop yields, and provide farmers with a sustainable income.

The success of the **Djan-Djan project** has inspired similar initiatives across the country and has proven that permaculture can be an effective method for regenerating the land, enhancing resilience to climate change, and improving food security.

4. Urban Farming: Bringing Agriculture to Cities

Urban farming refers to the practice of growing food within urban environments, whether through community gardens, rooftop farms, or indoor vertical farming. As cities grow and agricultural land becomes scarcer, urban farming offers an innovative solution for local food production that can help reduce food miles and improve food security.

Key benefits of urban farming include:

- **Food sovereignty:** Urban farming can provide cities with a more resilient food supply by reducing reliance on long supply chains and promoting local production of fresh, healthy food.
- **Waste reduction:** Many urban farms utilize organic waste from cities (such as food scraps and yard trimmings) to create compost or composting toilets, reducing waste sent to landfills.
- **Community engagement:** Urban farms create spaces for people to engage with food production and learn about sustainable agriculture. These farms can also serve as community hubs, improving social cohesion and public health.

Real-World Example: Brooklyn Grange in New York City

Brooklyn Grange operates one of the largest rooftop farms in the world, growing vegetables, herbs, and flowers on rooftops across New York City. The farm serves both as a local food source and as a model for urban farming in densely populated areas. Brooklyn Grange has demonstrated how cities can integrate agriculture into their infrastructure, contributing to food security, reducing food miles, and providing educational opportunities about sustainable farming. The farm's success has led to the growth of similar rooftop farms in other cities across the U.S. and globally.

Urban farming can be a part of the solution to urban food insecurity, providing fresh, local produce to city dwellers while promoting sustainable urban living.

From regenerative farming techniques that restore soil health and sequester carbon, to agroforestry systems that integrate trees with crops for enhanced biodiversity, to permaculture approaches that design closed-loop systems of food production, these models show us that a sustainable agricultural future is not only possible but already being realized in many places. Moreover, urban farming demonstrates how sustainability can be integrated into cities, which are increasingly becoming the epicenters of global population growth.

What these examples highlight is that sustainable agriculture is not a one-size-fits-all approach. It encompasses a wide variety of techniques and models tailored to local conditions, climates, and cultures. By supporting and scaling these innovative farming systems, we can address environmental degradation, restore ecosystems, and ensure that future generations have access to healthy, sustainable food. The key now is to expand these efforts globally, invest in research and education, and create the policies and incentives that will allow these models to thrive on a much larger scale.

Food Security and Sustainability

When we talk about food security, we are referring to the ability of people to access sufficient, safe, and nutritious food to meet their dietary needs and food preferences. This is a critical issue, particularly as the global population continues to rise and climate change begins to disrupt traditional food systems. Yet, food security is not just about food availability—it's also about sustainability. The question we must ask is not just how we can feed the world but how we can feed it in a way that doesn't compromise the ability of future generations to do the same.

The challenge of achieving food security is compounded by the environmental crises we face, including soil degradation, water scarcity, and climate change. Industrial agriculture, which relies heavily on monoculture farming, synthetic fertilizers, and pesticides, is a major contributor to these issues. Its practices degrade soil health, pollute water supplies, and emit greenhouse gases that drive climate change, which in turn threatens agricultural productivity. The result is a vicious cycle: as the environment deteriorates, our ability to produce food becomes more uncertain, and food prices rise, exacerbating hunger and poverty.

So, what is the solution to this conundrum? The answer lies in sustainable agriculture—a model that prioritizes environmental stewardship while ensuring long-term food security. Sustainable farming methods that regenerate the soil, conserve water, and reduce reliance on fossil fuels not only mitigate environmental damage but also contribute to resilient food systems that can withstand the shocks of a changing climate.

The Link Between Sustainable Agriculture and Food Security

Sustainable agriculture and food security are deeply intertwined. A more sustainable food system is one that can meet the nutritional needs of all people, today and in the future, while respecting the planet's finite resources. Some of the ways sustainable agriculture directly supports food security include:

1. **Restoring   Soil   Health**
   Soil is the foundation of our food systems. Healthy, fertile soil is essential for growing nutritious crops, yet industrial farming practices have severely depleted soil quality worldwide. Practices like monoculture and excessive tilling strip away the soil's organic matter, leaving it prone to erosion and less able to retain water. This not only makes food production more vulnerable to climate change, but it also diminishes the land's ability to support long-term agricultural productivity.

Sustainable farming practices, such as crop rotation, cover cropping, and no-till farming, help restore and maintain soil health. These practices increase organic matter, improve soil structure, and enhance its ability to retain moisture, which in turn boosts crop resilience to droughts and extreme weather events. Healthy soil is also a natural carbon sink, helping to mitigate climate change—a double win for both the environment and future food security.

2. **Improving** **Water** **Management**
Water is another critical resource for food production, and as water scarcity becomes an increasingly urgent issue, the need for more efficient water management in agriculture is paramount. Conventional farming methods, with their reliance on large-scale irrigation and excessive water usage, exacerbate water shortages and lead to the depletion of vital water sources.

Sustainable agriculture can improve water use efficiency through practices such as drip irrigation, rainwater harvesting, and mulching. By reducing water waste and ensuring that water is used more effectively, these practices help maintain water supplies while increasing crop yields. Moreover, regenerative practices such as agroforestry, which integrates trees into farming systems, can improve water retention and reduce the risk of soil erosion, further ensuring that crops have access to the water they need to thrive.

3. **Enhancing** **Resilience** **to** **Climate** **Change**
Climate change is already affecting agricultural systems around the world, and its impact on food security is becoming increasingly apparent. Rising temperatures, altered precipitation patterns, and more frequent extreme weather events—such as droughts, floods, and heatwaves—are all threatening food production. In regions where agriculture is heavily dependent on predictable weather patterns, such changes are devastating.

Sustainable farming practices offer a solution by enhancing agricultural resilience. By diversifying crops, integrating agroecological principles, and focusing on soil health, farmers can create more resilient systems that can better withstand climate-related shocks. For example, diverse polycultures (growing a variety of crops together) are less susceptible to pest outbreaks, drought, and disease than monocultures. Similarly, agroforestry systems—where trees are integrated with crops—can create microclimates that buffer extreme weather conditions, such as heat waves and heavy rainfall.

4. **Supporting** **Local** **Food** **Systems**
One of the key advantages of sustainable agriculture is its ability to support local food systems. Industrial agriculture often relies on global supply chains that are vulnerable to disruptions, whether from political instability, natural disasters, or pandemics. These disruptions can lead to food shortages and price hikes, further exacerbating hunger and inequality.

Sustainable agriculture, by contrast, emphasizes local production and consumption, reducing dependence on distant markets. Local food systems are more resilient because they are less susceptible to the vulnerabilities of global trade networks. By supporting small-scale, regenerative farmers, we can build local economies, reduce food waste, and ensure that fresh, nutritious food is available to communities regardless of external shocks.

The Economic and Social Dimensions of Food Security

While environmental sustainability is the cornerstone of securing the future of food, the social and economic dimensions cannot be overlooked. A sustainable food system is also one that is economically viable for farmers and socially just for communities.

- **Small-Scale Farming:** Sustainable agriculture often benefits small-scale farmers who are more directly tied to their land and community. These farmers are less likely to adopt destructive practices that degrade the environment, as they rely on the long-term health of their land to maintain their livelihoods. Supporting small-scale farmers also ensures a more equitable food system, where food sovereignty—the right of communities to control their own food production—is at the forefront.

- **Fair Trade and Ethical Consumption:** Sustainable agriculture often goes hand-in-hand with fair trade practices. By choosing products that are sustainably grown and ethically sourced, consumers can support farmers who are committed to environmentally friendly practices and fair labor conditions. Ethical consumption not only benefits farmers but also helps ensure that communities around the world have access to fair wages, safe working conditions, and a more just food system.

The path to food security in the 21st century is inseparable from the need for sustainability. By shifting to agricultural systems that prioritize environmental health, resource efficiency, and resilience, we can ensure that we meet the nutritional needs of a growing global population without compromising the ability of future generations to do the same. Sustainable agriculture offers solutions to the challenges of climate change, soil degradation, and water scarcity, while also promoting fair and equitable access to food.

Sustainable agriculture is more than just a buzzword—it is a necessity for the survival of our planet and the future of humanity. As we've explored, the conventional methods of industrial farming are increasingly incompatible with the need to preserve the environment, combat climate change, and ensure that food is available to all people. However, sustainable agriculture provides a hopeful solution, one that can regenerate ecosystems, restore soil health, conserve water, and create resilient food systems that are better equipped to withstand the challenges of a rapidly changing world.

From regenerative farming to agroforestry, permaculture, and urban farming, the examples of sustainable agricultural practices are diverse and effective. These models not only provide tangible solutions to the environmental crises we face but also lay the groundwork for a more just, equitable, and resilient global food system.

Chapter 6

Deforestation
The Global Crisis of Forest Loss

Deforestation is one of the most pressing environmental crises of our time. The world's forests—particularly tropical rainforests—are vital to the health of the planet. They provide essential ecosystem services, regulate the global climate, maintain biodiversity, and support the livelihoods of millions of people. Yet, every year, millions of hectares of forest are lost, often with irreversible consequences.

Deforestation, the large-scale removal or destruction of forests, has profound impacts on the environment. It not only contributes to climate change by releasing vast amounts of stored carbon dioxide into the atmosphere, but it also endangers biodiversity, disrupts water cycles, and causes soil erosion. In this chapter, we will explore the far-reaching consequences of deforestation, focusing on the direct and indirect effects it has on the environment, communities, and global systems.

1. Climate Change: Forests as Carbon Sinks

Forests are often referred to as the "lungs of the Earth," as they absorb large amounts of carbon dioxide (CO_2) through the process of photosynthesis and store it in their biomass. This is one of the key ways forests mitigate climate change by helping to regulate atmospheric CO_2 levels. The trees in the world's forests store more than two-thirds of the planet's terrestrial carbon. When forests are destroyed or degraded—whether through logging, agriculture, or fires—they release this stored carbon back into the atmosphere, exacerbating global warming.

The tropical rainforests—such as the Amazon, Congo Basin, and Southeast Asian rainforests—are particularly important in this regard. These forests are home to an enormous amount of the world's carbon storage capacity. However, as these forests are cleared at an alarming rate for industrial agriculture (particularly cattle ranching, palm oil production, and soy farming), vast amounts of carbon are being released into the atmosphere, further intensifying climate change.

To put the scale of this problem into perspective, scientists estimate that tropical deforestation alone contributes to about 10-15% of global greenhouse gas emissions—more than the entire transportation sector. The continued loss of forests is thus both a driver and a consequence of climate change, creating a feedback loop where deforestation accelerates global warming, and in turn, global warming drives more forest loss through increased fires, droughts, and pests.

2. Biodiversity Loss: The Extinction Crisis

Forests are home to more than 80% of the planet's terrestrial species, making them critical for preserving global biodiversity. They provide habitats for countless plants, animals, and microorganisms, many of which are yet to be discovered. Deforestation and forest degradation lead directly to the loss of these habitats, pushing species toward extinction and endangering the delicate balance of ecosystems.

In tropical rainforests, the destruction of habitat is particularly devastating. Species that depend on these ecosystems often cannot survive when the forests are fragmented or completely destroyed. This is especially true for endemic species—organisms that are found nowhere else in the world. Once a forest disappears, these species have nowhere to go, and extinction becomes a real threat.

Real-life examples of biodiversity loss due to deforestation include:

- **The Amazon Rainforest:** Often referred to as the "world's lungs," the Amazon is home to an unparalleled diversity of life. Over the past few decades, deforestation driven by agriculture, logging, and mining has led to the destruction of vast swaths of this vital ecosystem. Species such as the jaguar, giant river otter, and Brazilian tapir have seen their habitats destroyed, and many are now considered vulnerable or endangered. A recent study found that the loss of forest in the Amazon has pushed the region into a "tipping point" where the rainforest could transition into a savannah-like ecosystem, with far-reaching consequences for biodiversity.

- **The Bornean Orangutan:** Habitat loss caused by palm oil plantations has led to a dramatic decline in the Bornean orangutan population. This species, found only on the islands of Borneo and Sumatra, is now critically endangered. With the continued expansion of palm oil production, which is a major driver of deforestation in Southeast Asia, the survival of the orangutan and many other species is at risk.

- **The Indonesian Rainforests:** The forests of Indonesia are home to some of the most biodiverse ecosystems on the planet. However, logging and land clearing for palm oil, rubber, and paper production have led to significant habitat loss. Species like the Sumatran tiger, orangutan, and rhinoceros are now on the brink of extinction, with fewer than 400 Sumatran tigers remaining in the wild.

Deforestation is thus a leading cause of the current biodiversity crisis—referred to as the Sixth Mass Extinction—as ecosystems that support millions of species are being destroyed at an unprecedented rate. The loss of these species not only reduces the world's natural heritage but also disrupts ecosystems that provide vital services, such as pollination, pest control, and nutrient cycling.

3. Disruption of the Water Cycle: Forests as Regulators of Hydrology

Forests play a critical role in regulating the global water cycle. Trees and plants take up large quantities of water from the soil and release it into the atmosphere through transpiration, a process that helps maintain cloud formation and rainfall patterns. By absorbing and releasing water, forests create a microclimate that regulates precipitation and prevents drought.

When forests are cleared, this delicate balance is upset. In tropical forests, for example, deforestation can reduce rainfall by up to 50%, creating conditions that are more prone to drought. This, in turn, affects agricultural productivity, increases the frequency of wildfires, and can lead to the desertification of entire regions.

A striking example of this can be seen in Brazil's Amazon Basin. The Amazon is a key player in the South American water cycle, with the forest producing significant rainfall that nourishes agriculture, hydropower, and the local population. As deforestation rates have increased in recent years, the region has begun experiencing more severe droughts and water shortages, which have had profound social and economic consequences.

The loss of forest cover in other regions, such as the Congo Basin and Southeast Asia, has similarly disrupted the water cycle, creating conditions that exacerbate flooding, landslides, and water scarcity, while undermining the agricultural productivity of these areas.

4. Soil Erosion and Degradation: The Cost of Deforestation

Another major environmental impact of deforestation is soil erosion. Forests play a critical role in protecting soil by preventing erosion through the root systems of trees and plants, which bind the soil together. When forests are cleared, the soil is left exposed to the elements, which leads to erosion by wind and water.

In tropical regions, where the soil is often shallow and nutrient-poor, the loss of forests can lead to rapid soil degradation. Once the protective layer of trees is removed, rainwater can wash away topsoil, rendering the land less fertile and incapable of supporting crops. In the worst-case scenarios, deforested areas can become desertified, turning once-fertile regions into barren wastelands.

For example, in parts of Sub-Saharan Africa and Central America, deforestation has been a major factor contributing to soil erosion and the desertification of once-productive agricultural land. As forests disappear, the land becomes less productive, leading to food insecurity and the displacement of communities.

The impacts of deforestation are vast and interconnected, touching nearly every aspect of life on Earth. Forests are not only carbon sinks, but they also play a crucial role in regulating climate, preserving biodiversity, supporting the water cycle, and preventing soil erosion. The destruction of forests has far-reaching consequences, from accelerating climate change to driving species extinction, and from disrupting local water systems to undermining the productivity of agricultural lands.

As we face the twin crises of climate change and biodiversity loss, it is clear that deforestation must be addressed as a central issue in any comprehensive environmental strategy. To protect the planet's future, it is imperative that we take urgent and coordinated action to halt deforestation and promote reforestation and sustainable land management practices. The health of our forests is the health of our planet, and their loss is not just a local or national problem—it is a global emergency.

The Industries Responsible for Deforestation

The destruction of the world's forests is not a natural phenomenon. It is driven by human activities, many of which are deeply entrenched in our global economic system. While deforestation is a complex issue with various causes, certain industries bear significant responsibility for driving forest loss. From agriculture to logging to mining, these industries fuel the demand for land, often at the expense of some of the most biodiverse ecosystems on the planet. In this section, we will explore the key industries that are primarily responsible for deforestation, as well as the economic and social pressures that perpetuate the destruction of forests.

1. Agriculture: The Leading Driver of Deforestation

The agriculture industry is the primary driver of global deforestation. According to the Food and Agriculture Organization (FAO), agriculture accounts for approximately 80% of global deforestation. This includes both large-scale commercial agriculture and subsistence farming, with the primary drivers being the demand for crops like soy, palm oil, cocoa, coffee, rubber, and corn, as well as the need for pastureland for livestock.

- **Cattle Ranching and Pasture Expansion**: One of the most significant contributors to deforestation, particularly in the Amazon Basin, is the expansion of cattle ranching. The demand for beef, driven by global consumption trends, has resulted in large swaths of rainforest being cleared to make way for grazing land. In Brazil, for example, pastureland for cattle accounts for around 60-70% of the total deforestation in the Amazon. As the global demand for beef continues to rise, so does the pressure on tropical forests to make way for more grazing land. In fact, the Amazon has been referred to as the "lungs of the Earth," as it plays a critical role in carbon sequestration and climate regulation. When these forests are cleared for cattle ranching, not only is carbon stored in trees released into the atmosphere, but the land is also left barren, with long-lasting ecological consequences.

- **Soy Production**: Soy is another major crop responsible for deforestation, particularly in the Amazon and Cerrado regions of Brazil. Soy is used in a wide range of products, including animal feed, oil, and processed food ingredients, with China and the European Union being major importers. Large tracts of tropical forests are cleared to make room for soy monocultures, which not only devastate biodiversity but also contribute to soil degradation. In some regions, such as the Gran Chaco in Argentina and Paraguay, vast forests are being replaced by industrial soy farms. While there have been some efforts to reduce deforestation linked to soy production through initiatives like the Soy Moratorium (a voluntary agreement between companies to halt soy production in recently deforested areas), enforcement is often lax, and illegal deforestation continues.

- **Palm Oil**: Palm oil, used in a wide array of products such as food, cosmetics, and biofuels, is one of the most controversial agricultural drivers of deforestation. The global demand for palm oil has led to the destruction of millions of hectares of tropical rainforests, particularly in Indonesia and Malaysia. Both countries are home to some of the world's most biodiverse rainforests, and their destruction is causing the loss of habitat for critically endangered species such as the Sumatran orangutan, tigers, and rhinos. Despite promises of sustainable palm oil production through the **Roundtable on Sustainable Palm Oil (RSPO)**, the reality is that much of the palm oil industry continues to drive illegal land clearing, often through the use of fire, which results in catastrophic environmental damage.

2. Logging: The Demand for Timber, Paper, and Palm Oil

Logging is another major industry responsible for deforestation, particularly in tropical regions, where forests are cleared to meet the global demand for timber, paper products, and other wood-based materials. Illegal logging is a significant driver of deforestation, as many tropical nations lack the enforcement mechanisms to prevent it. Logging often occurs in areas that are protected by law or in remote regions where the forest is difficult to monitor.

- **Timber and Paper**: The demand for timber for construction, furniture, and paper products has led to the depletion of forests, especially in regions like the Congo Basin, Southeast Asia, and Brazil. The clearing of forests for timber can lead to soil erosion, disrupt local hydrological cycles, and threaten the survival of local communities who rely on the forest for food, shelter, and traditional practices. Additionally, the paper industry—often fed by demand for newspapers, packaging, and office supplies—is a major contributor to deforestation.

- **Illegal Logging**: Illegal logging is one of the most insidious forms of deforestation. It is often driven by weak governance, corruption, and the vast demand for timber. Illegal logging operations are often unregulated and carried out with little regard for the long-term health of the forest or the rights of indigenous communities. This type of logging not only contributes to deforestation but also exacerbates social tensions, as local and indigenous communities fight to preserve their land and way of life.

3. Mining: The Destruction of Forests for Resources

The mining industry is a significant driver of deforestation, particularly in tropical regions rich in natural resources. Mining operations—whether for gold, diamonds, oil, or other minerals—require vast amounts of land, often leading to the clearing of large forested areas. In addition to deforestation, mining causes soil erosion, water pollution, and biodiversity loss.

- **Gold Mining**: In regions like the Amazon Basin, illegal gold mining is one of the most destructive forms of land use. Gold miners clear forested areas to create large open-pit mines, often using toxic chemicals like mercury to extract the gold. These activities destroy ecosystems, pollute rivers and streams, and displace indigenous peoples who depend on the forest for their livelihoods. In Brazil, the Amazon region has been heavily affected by gold mining, which contributes to both deforestation and water contamination.

- **Oil and Gas Extraction**: The oil and gas industry is another significant contributor to deforestation, particularly in places like the Congo Basin and the Amazon Rainforest. Oil companies clear forests to create infrastructure for drilling operations, pipelines, and access roads. The extraction process also often leads to soil and water pollution, while spills and leaks can devastate local ecosystems. In countries like Ecuador, the oil industry has caused extensive damage to the Amazonian rainforest, with indigenous communities suffering the loss of both their land and resources.

4. Infrastructure Development: Roads, Urbanization, and Industrial Expansion

Infrastructure development, including the construction of roads, highways, dams, and cities, is a less obvious but highly significant driver of deforestation. The construction of new roads, often in previously remote forested areas, facilitates access to previously untouched regions, leading to both legal and illegal logging, farming, and mining activities.

- **Roads and Access**: Roads are often the first step in clearing the way for agricultural expansion and logging. In the Amazon, for example, roads have opened up previously inaccessible forest areas, leading to a surge in land clearing for cattle ranching and soy farming. As roads expand, so too does the human footprint in forested areas, contributing to the rapid fragmentation of habitats and ecosystems.

- **Urban Expansion**: As global populations grow and urbanization continues, the demand for land for housing, industrial parks, and infrastructure projects increases. In rapidly developing regions such as Southeast Asia, this has led to the clearing of vast tracts of forest to accommodate expanding cities and industrial complexes.

5. The Role of Global Supply Chains and Trade

Behind the industries driving deforestation is a complex web of global supply chains. The demand for commodities like beef, palm oil, soy, timber, and rubber is not driven solely by local populations, but by consumers across the world. The power of multinational corporations to influence land use in developing countries cannot be overstated. The pressures of the global market are often so great that local governments and businesses are incentivized to prioritize short-term economic gains over long-term environmental sustainability.

The industries responsible for deforestation are powerful, global, and deeply embedded in the economic system. Agriculture, logging, mining, and infrastructure development are the primary culprits, with growing consumer demand for products like beef, palm oil, and timber driving much of the destruction. However, the consequences of deforestation extend far beyond the industries involved—they affect the global climate, biodiversity, and the livelihoods of millions of people. To tackle deforestation, we must address the root causes in these industries, advocating for sustainable practices, enforcing stronger environmental protections, and demanding transparency from companies across supply chains. Only by changing how we produce, consume, and trade can we hope to halt the widespread destruction of the world's forests.

Efforts to Combat Deforestation

Despite the alarming rates of deforestation worldwide, significant efforts have been made to combat this environmental crisis. From government policies and international agreements to grassroots movements and corporate responsibility initiatives, a variety of strategies are being employed to slow and even reverse the trend of forest loss. While these efforts face challenges, they provide hope that deforestation can be mitigated, and in some cases, forest restoration is possible. In this section, we will explore the most prominent efforts and the challenges they face.

1. International Agreements and Forest Protection Initiatives

One of the most effective ways to combat deforestation is through international cooperation. Global environmental agreements, such as the Paris Agreement on climate change, highlight the need to protect forests as part of the solution to global warming. Forests are essential carbon sinks, and protecting them is crucial to achieving climate targets. International initiatives aimed at reducing deforestation, such as REDD+ (Reducing Emissions from Deforestation and Forest Degradation), have become central to discussions on climate change and conservation.

- **REDD+:** REDD+ is a United Nations program that provides financial incentives to developing countries to reduce deforestation and forest degradation. It aims to create a system in which countries are compensated for conserving their forests and limiting deforestation. The program encourages forest conservation by linking it to global climate finance and carbon markets, giving countries an economic reason to preserve forests instead of clearing them for agriculture or industry. Although the program has had some success in slowing deforestation in places like Indonesia, challenges remain, particularly related to governance, transparency, and ensuring that the benefits of REDD+ reach local communities.

- **The Paris Agreement and Forests**: While the Paris Agreement focuses primarily on reducing greenhouse gas emissions, it also recognizes the importance of forests in mitigating climate change. Article 5 of the agreement explicitly calls for "enhanced support to reduce emissions from deforestation and forest degradation." Many countries have included forest protection as part of their climate commitments, and some have made significant strides. However, the challenge lies in implementation. Achieving forest protection and climate goals simultaneously requires more than just policy; it requires local and national actions that involve sustainable land use, enforcement of laws, and addressing the root causes of deforestation.

2. National Legislation and Policy Change

In many countries, national laws and regulations aimed at protecting forests and curbing illegal logging have been enacted. While these policies vary widely, some have had measurable success in slowing deforestation rates and promoting sustainable land management practices.

- **Brazil's Forest Code**: Brazil, home to the world's largest tropical rainforest, has made significant strides in reducing deforestation in the Amazon over the last two decades. The Brazilian government implemented a range of measures to curb deforestation, including satellite monitoring of deforestation hotspots, the creation of protected areas, and stricter enforcement of logging laws. **The Forest Code,** revised in 2012, set aside more land for conservation and required landowners in the Amazon to restore degraded lands. Between 2004 and 2012, Brazil saw a remarkable 80% drop in Amazon deforestation. However, deforestation has surged again in recent years, particularly under the leadership of former president Jair Bolsonaro, who rolled back environmental protections and encouraged illegal logging and land grabs in the Amazon. This demonstrates how easily progress can be undone when political will shifts.

- **Indonesia's Moratorium on New Forest Concessions**: Indonesia, another country with vast tropical forests, has made strides in addressing deforestation. In 2011, the Indonesian government imposed a moratorium on new forest concessions, halting the granting of permits for new palm oil plantations and logging activities in primary forests and peatlands. The government also established peatland restoration programs, recognizing the need to restore damaged ecosystems to mitigate the impacts of climate change. However, implementation remains a challenge, as illegal logging and land conversion for palm oil and other crops continue in many areas, particularly in Sumatra and Borneo.

3. Corporate Responsibility and the Role of Industry

Corporations, particularly those in industries directly linked to deforestation, are increasingly being held accountable for their role in forest destruction. In response to consumer pressure, international environmental organizations, and government regulations, many companies are adopting sustainability pledges and committing to zero-deforestation supply chains.

- **The Roundtable on Sustainable Palm Oil (RSPO)**: In response to the rampant deforestation driven by palm oil production, the RSPO was established in 2004. This certification body sets standards for sustainable palm oil production and aims to eliminate deforestation in the supply chain. Companies like Nestlé, Unilever, and Cargill have made commitments to source only certified sustainable palm oil. While the RSPO has been instrumental in raising awareness about the environmental impact of palm oil, critics argue that it does not go far enough in enforcing standards and preventing land grabbing or illegal deforestation linked to palm oil production. Despite these challenges, the RSPO is one of the leading examples of how industry can take steps toward reducing its environmental footprint.

- **Sustainable Soy and Cattle Agreements**: Several agreements have been put in place to reduce deforestation linked to the production of soy and beef. For example, in Brazil, the Soy Moratorium, established in 2006, is a voluntary commitment by companies not to purchase soy from areas that have been newly deforested in the Amazon. Similarly, the **Cattle Agreement (also known as the Amazon Beef Pact)** aims to stop the trade of beef linked to deforestation in the Amazon. While these initiatives have been successful in curbing deforestation in some areas, illegal deforestation and supply chain loopholes remain a significant challenge. The effectiveness of such corporate pledges is often undermined by the lack of enforcement mechanisms and transparency.

4. Grassroots Movements and Community-Driven Solutions

While governments and corporations play a large role in combating deforestation, local communities and grassroots movements are also leading efforts to protect forests. Indigenous communities, in particular, have long been at the forefront of forest conservation, as their livelihoods are directly tied to the health of the forests they call home.

- **Indigenous Land Rights**: One of the most effective ways to combat deforestation is by securing land rights for indigenous peoples. Studies have shown that forests on indigenous lands are often better protected and less likely to be deforested compared to those under government control. In Brazil, the Kayapo and Xingu indigenous groups have been successful in resisting illegal logging and land grabs, preserving vast tracts of Amazon rainforest. Empowering indigenous communities with legal land rights is a powerful strategy for forest conservation.

- **Community Forestry Projects**: In many countries, community forestry initiatives are helping local populations manage and protect forests sustainably. In Nepal, for example, community-managed forests have led to reforestation and sustainable wood harvesting, benefiting both local communities and the environment. These projects not only reduce deforestation but also provide economic benefits, improve biodiversity, and strengthen social cohesion.

5. Reforestation and Restoration Initiatives

In addition to preventing deforestation, reforestation and forest restoration are critical components of global efforts to restore ecosystems and combat climate change. Reforestation refers to the process of replanting trees in areas where forests have been lost, while restoration focuses on repairing degraded ecosystems to bring them back to health.

- **The Bonn Challenge**: An international initiative, the Bonn Challenge aims to restore 350 million hectares of deforested and degraded land by 2030. The challenge is a collaborative effort between governments, businesses, and civil society to reforest areas and restore landscapes. Several countries, including Ethiopia, Brazil, and Mexico, have made significant commitments to restoring degraded land, providing a model for other nations to follow.

- **The Great Green Wall**: In Africa, the Great Green Wall is an ambitious reforestation project designed to combat desertification and restore the Sahel region's ecosystems. The initiative aims to plant a wall of trees spanning across the Sahel, from Senegal to Djibouti, in an effort to improve soil health, create jobs, and restore ecosystems in one of the world's most vulnerable regions.

Efforts to combat deforestation are diverse and multifaceted, involving international cooperation, national policies, corporate responsibility, community-driven initiatives, and large-scale restoration programs. While challenges remain, these efforts provide a blueprint for what is possible if the global community takes coordinated and meaningful action. Protecting the world's forests requires a combination of strong governance, accountable industries, and empowered local communities. The fight against deforestation is far from over, but the momentum for change is growing. The future of our forests depends on all of us—governments, corporations, activists, and individuals—working together to safeguard these vital ecosystems for future generations.

Chapter 7

The Controversial Solutions
The Case for Hemp Cultivation

Hemp has long been a misunderstood and undervalued crop, often overshadowed by its more controversial relative, marijuana. Yet, beyond its association with cannabis culture, hemp has a rich history as a versatile and environmentally friendly resource. In recent years, hemp is emerging as a critical component of the movement toward sustainability and the fight against climate change. As the world confronts environmental crises such as deforestation, soil degradation, and the need for sustainable materials, hemp presents an opportunity to address these issues in a unique and scalable way. From building materials to biofuels, textiles to food, hemp offers a wide range of products that can be produced in ways that have minimal environmental impact.

1. A High-Yield, Low-Impact Crop

Hemp is an incredibly efficient crop that requires little water, no pesticides, and can thrive in a variety of soil types. Its rapid growth rate makes it an ideal option for agricultural production, as it can be harvested in as little as 3-4 months. Hemp's deep root system helps prevent soil erosion, and it can even improve soil health by promoting bioremediation—the process by which plants help to clean up pollutants in the soil. This makes hemp an excellent crop for areas that have suffered from overuse, erosion, or contamination.

- **Water Efficiency**: Unlike crops like cotton or corn, which require large amounts of water, hemp is known for its drought-resistant qualities. It can thrive with minimal irrigation, making it an ideal crop for regions facing water scarcity. The United Nations Food and Agriculture Organization (FAO) has pointed out that hemp is one of the most water-efficient crops, requiring far less water than conventional cash crops, such as cotton or tobacco. Hemp's ability to grow in areas with limited water resources could play a crucial role in addressing water scarcity issues in many parts of the world.

- **Soil Health and Regeneration**: Hemp's deep, strong roots are excellent for soil regeneration. They break up compacted soils and promote aeration, which improves water infiltration and root growth for subsequent crops. Additionally, hemp has been shown to be effective in remediating soil that has been contaminated with heavy metals or toxins. The plant absorbs and neutralizes these pollutants, leaving the soil in better condition for future agricultural use. This makes hemp a valuable tool for restoring degraded and polluted land.

- **Carbon Sequestration**: Like all plants, hemp absorbs carbon dioxide through photosynthesis, helping to mitigate climate change by storing carbon in its fibers and roots. In fact, hemp is considered one of the most carbon-negative crops— meaning that it captures more carbon than is emitted during its cultivation, processing, and production. According to studies, one hectare of hemp can absorb around 15 tons of CO2 per year, making it a powerful tool in the global fight against climate change.

2. Hemp as a Source of Sustainable Materials

One of the most compelling arguments for hemp is its potential to replace unsustainable materials used in a wide range of industries, from construction to fashion to packaging. Hemp fibers are incredibly durable and can be used to make products that are both biodegradable and environmentally friendly. The versatility of hemp makes it an ideal candidate to replace traditional materials that contribute to deforestation, pollution, and fossil fuel dependency.

- **Hemp as a Building Material**: Hemp has long been used in construction, particularly in the form of hempcrete, a lightweight, insulating material made from hemp fibers mixed with lime and water. Hempcrete is both fire-resistant and mold-resistant, making it a durable and safe alternative to traditional building materials like concrete and insulation. Not only does hempcrete have a much lower carbon footprint than conventional building materials, but it also contributes to energy efficiency in buildings, reducing heating and cooling costs. Additionally, hemp-based materials are biodegradable, meaning they won't contribute to the growing problem of construction waste once they've reached the end of their useful life.

- **Hemp Textiles and Clothing**: Hemp fibers have been used for thousands of years to make fabric and clothing. Today, hemp textiles are experiencing a resurgence due to growing consumer demand for sustainable fashion. Hemp fibers are naturally strong, durable, and biodegradable, making them an ideal material for clothing, shoes, and accessories. Compared to cotton, hemp requires far less water, pesticides, and synthetic fertilizers to grow, making it a more sustainable option for the fashion industry. Hemp fabrics are also naturally resistant to mold, mildew, and ultraviolet light, meaning they can last longer and require less frequent replacement, reducing textile waste.

- **Hemp-Based Plastics**: Hemp is being explored as an alternative to petroleum-based plastics. Hemp fibers can be processed into biodegradable plastics that can be used in everything from packaging to automotive parts to consumer goods. Hemp-based plastics have a much lower environmental impact than traditional plastics, which are often made from nonrenewable fossil fuels and take hundreds of years to break down in the environment. In addition to being biodegradable, hemp plastics can also be recycled and composted, contributing to a more sustainable and circular economy.

- **Biofuels and Hemp-Based Energy**: Hemp can also be processed into biofuels, including hemp oil and ethanol, which can be used to power vehicles or generate electricity. Biofuels derived from hemp are considered more sustainable than fossil fuels, as they are renewable, carbon-neutral, and can be produced with fewer environmental impacts. Unlike traditional biofuels made from food crops like corn or soy, which can contribute to food insecurity and land-use conflicts, hemp is a non-food crop that does not compete with agricultural land used for food production.

3. Hemp as a Health and Food Source

Hemp is not just a sustainable industrial resource—it also has nutritional value. The seeds of the hemp plant, often referred to as hemp hearts, are a rich source of protein, essential fatty acids, vitamins, and minerals. Hemp oil, extracted from the seeds, is also known for its health benefits, including anti-inflammatory properties and high levels of omega-3 and omega-6 fatty acids. As demand for plant-based and sustainable food sources grows, hemp offers a nutritious and environmentally friendly alternative to other protein-rich crops, such as soy.

- **Nutritional Benefits of Hemp Seeds**: Hemp seeds are a complete protein, meaning they contain all nine essential amino acids that the human body cannot produce on its own. They are also high in fiber and contain vitamin E, magnesium, iron, and zinc. Hemp seeds can be added to smoothies, salads, and baked goods or consumed as a snack. Hemp oil, which is pressed from the seeds, is often used as a dietary supplement for its anti-inflammatory properties and its ability to support heart health and brain function.

- **Sustainable Food Source**: As the global population grows and the demand for sustainable food sources increases, hemp offers an alternative to resource-intensive crops like soy and livestock. Hemp requires far fewer resources to produce, making it a more sustainable option for feeding people in an environmentally friendly way.

Hemp is a remarkable crop that holds the potential to transform several key industries, from construction and textiles to food production and energy. Its environmental benefits, such as water efficiency, carbon sequestration, and soil regeneration, make it a powerful ally in the fight against climate change. Moreover, its ability to replace unsustainable materials in various sectors, combined with its potential as a healthful food source, positions hemp as a multifaceted solution to some of the planet's most pressing environmental challenges. As more people and industries embrace hemp, it is poised to play a central role in the shift toward a more sustainable and circular economy. However, to fully unlock its potential, there must be greater support for hemp cultivation, investment in infrastructure, and the removal of regulatory barriers that have historically hindered its widespread adoption. The future of hemp could be the key to creating a more sustainable and equitable world.

The History of Hemp Regulation

Despite its vast potential, the widespread use of hemp has been hampered by a long and controversial history of regulation, particularly in the 20th century. What is often overlooked is that hemp has been cultivated for thousands of years, revered by many ancient civilizations for its versatility as a material for ropes, textiles, and paper, as well as for its nutritional and medicinal benefits. In fact, hemp's history of use predates written records, with archaeological evidence indicating it was used in ancient China, Egypt, and Mesopotamia.

However, in the modern era, hemp's path took a drastic turn, primarily due to its association with marijuana and the growing political and economic interests that sought to control or eliminate it. The regulation and eventual criminalization of hemp have had a profound impact on its production, research, and perception in society. Understanding this history is essential to comprehending why hemp is only now experiencing a resurgence as a sustainable resource.

1. The Rise of Hemp in Early America

Hemp was one of the earliest crops cultivated in North America, and it was highly prized for its strength and versatility. The early American colonies were encouraged to grow hemp for use in shipbuilding, textile production, and as a source of paper and twine. In fact, hemp was considered so important that farmers were sometimes required to grow it. In the late 1700s and early 1800s, the U.S. government even offered bounties for hemp production, and figures like George Washington and Thomas Jefferson grew hemp on their plantations.

Hemp was recognized as a vital resource for the nascent American economy, especially for producing materials like sails and ropes for the booming shipping industry. This period marked the beginning of a long tradition of hemp cultivation in the United States, which continued into the 19th century, when hemp was used for everything from clothing to currency.

2. The Stigmatization of Hemp and the Rise of Marijuana Prohibition

The shift from hemp's widespread acceptance to its criminalization began in the early 20th century, with the growing stigmatization of marijuana—a product derived from the cannabis plant. As cannabis consumption increased in the United States, particularly among Mexican immigrants and the African-American community in the early 1900s, marijuana was increasingly associated with criminal behavior and social unrest. This fear and prejudice against marijuana were amplified by the rise of racism, xenophobia, and political agendas that sought to control marginalized communities.

In the 1930s, the U.S. government launched a coordinated campaign to demonize marijuana and its users. The most notorious figure in this campaign was Harry Anslinger, the first commissioner of the Federal Bureau of Narcotics, who championed the criminalization of both marijuana and hemp. Anslinger's efforts culminated in the passage of the Marihuana Tax Act of 1937, which effectively made hemp production illegal by imposing heavy restrictions on its cultivation and use.

The Marihuana Tax Act classified hemp alongside marijuana, despite the fact that the two plants differ in their chemical composition. Marijuana was linked to psychoactive properties due to its high levels of THC (tetrahydrocannabinol), while hemp contains negligible levels of THC, making it unsuitable for recreational drug use. However, the public's fear and misinformation about marijuana led to the broad criminalization of all cannabis plants, including industrial hemp.

This law created an immediate setback for hemp production in the United States, essentially rendering it unprofitable and dangerous to grow. It also set the stage for the stigmatization of hemp as a dangerous substance, equating it with illegal drug use.

3. World War II and the Temporary Resurgence of Hemp

In the 1940s, during World War II, the United States found itself facing a severe shortage of raw materials, particularly for military supplies like rope and parachutes. In response, the government recognized the strategic value of hemp and launched a program called "Hemp for Victory," encouraging farmers to grow hemp again for the war effort. The U.S. government provided subsidies and training for farmers to grow hemp, and the crop was used extensively to produce essential military materials, including cordage, uniform fabrics, and parachutes.

However, once the war ended, and hemp's military utility was no longer needed, the government quickly reverted to its previous stance of discouraging hemp production. The fear of marijuana and its social stigma overshadowed any pragmatic use of the crop, and hemp was once again suppressed. By the 1950s, hemp cultivation was virtually eliminated from the U.S. agricultural landscape.

4. The Controlled Substances Act and the End of Legal Hemp Cultivation

The final blow to legal hemp production came in 1970, with the passage of the Controlled Substances Act, which classified all forms of cannabis, including industrial hemp, as a Schedule I controlled substance. This law placed hemp under the same legal restrictions as marijuana, effectively banning its cultivation in the United States. Despite hemp's longstanding history as a non-psychoactive crop, the association with marijuana was enough to eliminate hemp from mainstream agricultural practices.

This categorization meant that hemp farmers were unable to access the legal protections, subsidies, and markets available to other crops. It also prevented the exploration of hemp's environmental and economic benefits, as research into the plant was stifled. The lack of legal hemp farming in the U.S. led to a dependence on foreign imports, primarily from countries like Canada and China, which continued to grow hemp legally.

5. The Modern Hemp Resurgence and Changing Regulations

It wasn't until the 1990s and early 2000s that the push for hemp legalization began to gain momentum again. Advocates for industrial hemp began to draw attention to its environmental and economic benefits, especially its potential as a sustainable resource in the face of climate change and the depletion of natural resources.

The first significant legislative breakthrough came with the 1999 Farm Bill, which legalized the cultivation of hemp for research purposes. This allowed a limited number of states and universities to begin studying hemp's potential as an industrial crop. However, this was still far from a nationwide policy shift, and legal hemp production remained largely confined to pilot programs and small-scale research.

The major turning point came with the passage of the 2018 Farm Bill, which removed hemp from the list of controlled substances and legalized its cultivation on a national level. This bill defined hemp as cannabis with less than 0.3% THC, allowing for the commercial cultivation of the crop for industrial purposes. The legalization of hemp spurred a wave of new interest and investment in the plant, leading to a rapid expansion of the hemp industry across the U.S. since 2019, particularly in states like Colorado, Kentucky, and Oregon.

The legal landscape for hemp is still evolving, with states continuing to implement their own regulations and restrictions. The market for hemp-derived products, including CBD oil, hemp-based textiles, biofuels, and construction materials, has exploded, providing new opportunities for farmers, entrepreneurs, and researchers. However, challenges remain, particularly in terms of market instability, crop quality control, and the continued stigma surrounding the cannabis plant as a whole.

6. The Global Perspective on Hemp Regulation

Globally, hemp is facing a similar regulatory renaissance. In Canada, hemp has been legally cultivated since 1998, and the country has emerged as one of the world leaders in hemp production. The European Union also legalized hemp cultivation for industrial purposes in the 1990s, and many EU countries, including France, Germany, and the Netherlands, have since invested in hemp-based industries.

Countries like China and Russia have long maintained hemp cultivation programs, producing large quantities of hemp fiber and seeds for global markets. However, despite this, the U.S. remains a key player in hemp's potential market, and its resurgence is being watched closely by international agricultural and environmental policy experts.

The regulation of hemp has undergone a significant transformation from being an essential crop to a criminalized and stigmatized plant, and now back to a crop of increasing promise for a sustainable future. The story of hemp regulation is one of political manipulation, misinformation, and shifting societal attitudes, which have prevented hemp from reaching its full potential for much of the 20th century. With the recent legalization and growing awareness of its environmental and economic benefits, hemp is poised for a major comeback. As policies continue to evolve, and the public continues to demand more sustainable and eco-friendly solutions, hemp stands as one of the most promising crops to lead the charge toward a more sustainable and resilient future.

Arguments For and Against Large-Scale Hemp Cultivation

Hemp is widely considered one of the most sustainable crops available today, offering a broad array of environmental, economic, and social benefits. However, as with any large-scale agricultural initiative, the push for widespread hemp cultivation is not without its challenges and criticisms. The debate surrounding large-scale hemp farming involves both passionate advocacy for its potential to drive sustainability and equally passionate concerns about its potential risks and unintended consequences.

1. Arguments For Large-Scale Hemp Cultivation

Environmental Benefits:

The most compelling argument for large-scale hemp cultivation revolves around its ability to support environmental sustainability. Hemp is a carbon-negative crop, meaning it absorbs more carbon dioxide than it emits during cultivation and processing. As the world faces the accelerating effects of climate change, scaling up hemp production could significantly contribute to reducing atmospheric CO_2 levels. It has been shown that one hectare of hemp can absorb up to 15 tons of CO_2 annually, making it an excellent tool for carbon sequestration.

Additionally, hemp can play a crucial role in soil regeneration. Hemp's deep root system helps prevent soil erosion, improves water retention, and can remediate contaminated soils through a process known as phytoremediation, where the plant absorbs harmful pollutants like heavy metals from the earth. For regions suffering from degraded or contaminated soil, hemp offers a natural and low-cost solution for environmental restoration.

Economic Benefits and Job Creation:

Large-scale hemp cultivation has the potential to create a wealth of economic opportunities. The hemp industry could generate thousands of green jobs in farming, processing, research, manufacturing, and retail sectors. As demand for sustainable products increases, industries such as bioplastics, hempcrete (hemp-based building materials), textiles, and biofuels could drive new growth. Given hemp's versatility, its market spans a variety of industries, from construction to food, cosmetics, automotive manufacturing, and energy.

In addition to creating jobs, large-scale hemp farming can also provide an income stream for farmers, especially in regions where conventional crops are failing due to climate change or land degradation. Hemp's relatively low input requirements—such as minimal pesticide use, fewer water resources, and limited fertilizer needs—make it an attractive alternative to traditional crops like cotton and tobacco.

Sustainable Agriculture:

Hemp could be a cornerstone crop in transitioning toward sustainable agricultural practices. As the agricultural sector faces increasing pressure to reduce its carbon footprint and minimize environmental damage, hemp's low-impact cultivation methods present a viable option for sustainable farming. It's naturally resistant to pests, reducing the need for harmful chemical pesticides. Furthermore, it can grow on a wide range of soils and climates, making it a resilient crop in the face of changing environmental conditions.

Biofuel Potential:

Hemp's potential to serve as a biofuel crop is another critical aspect of its argument for large-scale cultivation. Hemp can be converted into hemp oil and ethanol, which can be used to generate energy and reduce reliance on fossil fuels. Given the global push for cleaner, renewable energy sources, hemp could play an important role in the transition to a green economy by providing a sustainable, alternative energy resource that can be grown domestically, reducing dependence on foreign oil.

2. Arguments Against Large-Scale Hemp Cultivation

Land Use and Environmental Impact of Monoculture:

One of the key concerns about large-scale hemp cultivation is the potential environmental harm of cultivating hemp as a monoculture. While hemp itself is a low-maintenance, sustainable crop, the pressures of large-scale production could lead to the use of intensive farming practices that prioritize profit over sustainability. In some regions, monoculture farming—growing the same crop year after year—has led to soil depletion, loss of biodiversity, and ecosystem imbalance. If hemp were to be grown on vast expanses of land, its overproduction could pose risks of land degradation, especially if proper crop rotation and soil management practices aren't implemented.

Additionally, there are concerns that large-scale hemp farming could result in the displacement of other important crops. While hemp is often praised for its low water use, its large-scale cultivation may still compete with food crops for land and water resources. If hemp farming becomes too dominant in certain regions, it could exacerbate the issue of food insecurity, especially in areas already struggling with agricultural sustainability.

Economic Risks and Market Instability:

The hemp market is still in its early stages of growth, and large-scale cultivation poses risks due to the volatility of the hemp industry. Prices for hemp products—such as CBD oil, hemp textiles, and bioplastics—are still fluctuating and vulnerable to changes in consumer demand, regulatory frameworks, and market supply. A rapid expansion in hemp farming could result in oversupply, driving prices down and potentially destabilizing the market. Without careful regulation and management of supply and demand, farmers could face financial hardships if the market for hemp products crashes or fails to meet expectations.

Furthermore, as hemp is still a relatively new crop for many regions, the infrastructure required for processing and distribution is limited and expensive to build. From harvesting equipment to processing mills and manufacturing facilities, the hemp industry needs substantial investment in infrastructure, and its growth depends on coordinated efforts between farmers, policymakers, and private enterprises. Without such investment, the promise of large-scale hemp production may not be fully realized.

Regulatory and Legal Uncertainties:

While hemp cultivation has been legalized in many countries, including the United States, the legal landscape is still evolving. The ambiguity between hemp and marijuana remains a significant hurdle, as hemp is still associated with cannabis in the public mind. In some countries, there are stringent rules governing the THC content of hemp, which complicates the regulatory framework for hemp growers. Farmers may also face difficulty in accessing financial services, including insurance or loans, due to the lingering stigma surrounding the cannabis industry.

The patchwork of regulations at the state, national, and international levels can create uncertainty for both farmers and businesses, which could undermine large-scale hemp farming initiatives. Consistency in laws and a clear path to commercial cultivation are essential for hemp to become a mainstream agricultural product.

The Stigma and Public Perception:

Despite recent progress, the stigma surrounding cannabis remains a significant barrier to the widespread adoption of hemp farming. The lingering association between hemp and marijuana means that public perception of hemp may remain negative or misunderstood, particularly in areas with less exposure to the economic and environmental benefits of hemp cultivation. This stigma may also lead to resistance among policymakers, potential investors, and consumers, all of whom play a role in hemp's success as a sustainable resource.

The arguments for and against large-scale hemp cultivation highlight both its enormous potential and the challenges that must be navigated to fully realize its benefits. Hemp offers significant environmental advantages, from carbon sequestration to soil regeneration, and its economic potential in creating jobs and sustainable products is equally compelling. However, like any large-scale agricultural initiative, it requires careful management to avoid the pitfalls of monoculture farming, market instability, and regulatory uncertainty.

In the end, the success of large-scale hemp cultivation depends not just on embracing its many benefits but also on addressing the challenges that come with it. Proper regulation, support for infrastructure development, and careful management of its environmental impacts will be key in unlocking hemp's true potential as a sustainable and valuable resource for the future.

Hemp stands at the crossroads of environmental sustainability and economic opportunity. Its versatility as a crop, combined with its potential to contribute to a wide range of industries—from renewable energy and bioplastics to construction materials and nutrition—positions it as a powerful tool for addressing the environmental crises of our time. Yet, the history of hemp regulation and the ongoing debates about large-scale cultivation show that its widespread adoption will not be without obstacles. The need for continued research, careful policy development, and public education remains crucial if hemp is to reach its full potential.

As we move toward a more sustainable future, hemp could be the linchpin of a green revolution that transforms not only agriculture but also entire industries. However, its success will depend on how we balance its potential for positive change with the careful, responsible management of its cultivation and use. Only then can hemp fully live up to its promise as a cornerstone crop for a sustainable, carbon-neutral world.

Chapter 8

Environmental Jobs and Education Building the Workforce for the Green Economy

As the world faces the urgent challenge of addressing climate change and environmental degradation, a critical yet often overlooked component of the solution lies in the creation of green jobs—employment opportunities that not only contribute to environmental sustainability but also support the transition to a greener economy. The need for green jobs is not just about addressing the ecological crisis; it is also about meeting the growing demand for clean energy, sustainable agriculture, and environmental restoration while simultaneously providing meaningful work for millions of people.

The green economy is not a distant ideal; it is already here, and it is expanding at an unprecedented rate. According to the International Labour Organization (ILO), an estimated 24 million new jobs could be created worldwide by 2030 through investments in sustainable industries such as renewable energy, energy efficiency, waste management, and sustainable agriculture. The transition to a greener economy is already underway, and the demand for skilled workers in fields like solar energy, wind energy, electric vehicle manufacturing, sustainable construction, and environmental consulting is growing rapidly.

However, this surge in demand for green jobs presents both a tremendous opportunity and a significant challenge. The opportunity lies in the chance to reshape economies and communities, to create new industries and sectors that can both drive economic growth and help mitigate the devastating impacts of climate change. The challenge is in the education, training, and upskilling required to prepare the workforce for these new jobs, especially as traditional sectors are disrupted or rendered obsolete by new technologies and climate policies.

1. Transitioning from Traditional Industries to Green Jobs

One of the central reasons for the need for green jobs is the transition away from carbon-intensive industries like fossil fuels, industrial agriculture, and deforestation. As the world shifts toward clean energy sources like solar, wind, and hydropower, many of the jobs that have traditionally powered economies—coal mining, oil extraction, gas drilling, and the fossil fuel-powered automobile industry—are on the decline. This transition presents a significant challenge, especially for the millions of workers in these sectors who will find themselves displaced by new technologies and evolving market demands.

But the transition from traditional industries to green jobs is also an opportunity to reimagine economies, create better employment options, and reduce inequality. Renewable energy, for example, can provide a more decentralized, community-based model of energy generation, shifting control away from fossil fuel giants and placing it in the hands of local communities. Workers previously employed in coal mines or oil rigs can be retrained to work in solar panel installation, wind turbine maintenance, or battery storage technology—jobs that are cleaner, safer, and often higher-paying in the long term.

One study by the Center for American Progress estimated that transitioning to clean energy in the United States could generate nearly 25 million new jobs by 2030, outpacing the number of jobs lost in the fossil fuel industry. But to achieve this, significant investments in job retraining programs, community-based employment initiatives, and government-backed support are essential.

2. Addressing the Growing Demand for Renewable Energy Workers

Among the most pressing needs in the green job sector is the demand for skilled workers in renewable energy industries. The global push to reduce greenhouse gas emissions has led to a boom in the renewable energy sector, which is already the fastest-growing part of the energy industry. According to the International Renewable Energy Agency (IRENA), global renewable energy employment reached 12 million jobs in 2020 and is expected to grow exponentially in the coming years.

Within the renewable energy sector, the demand for workers spans a wide range of specializations, including solar photovoltaic (PV) technicians, wind turbine technicians, energy auditors, battery storage experts, electric vehicle (EV) technicians, and energy engineers. These jobs require specialized knowledge and technical expertise, meaning that skills training and education are key to meeting the demand for workers in this sector.

As governments and companies ramp up investments in solar, wind, and other renewable energy technologies, it is essential to ensure that workers have the necessary skills to meet the challenges of an evolving energy landscape. Programs that provide hands-on training and certification in renewable energy technologies, such as solar panel installation, wind farm maintenance, and electric vehicle servicing, will be critical in filling this gap. Community colleges, trade schools, and vocational training programs must adapt quickly to meet the increasing demand for these skills.

At the same time, it's important to ensure that workers in these fields are not only technically trained but also equipped with the knowledge of sustainability practices, green building principles, and climate science. This holistic approach to education and training will ensure that workers can contribute to broader environmental goals while also securing stable, high-quality employment.

3. The Role of Government and Private Sector in Job Creation

While the demand for green jobs is growing, it's important to recognize that creating these jobs requires both public policy and private sector investment. Governments play a key role in shaping the green economy through policy incentives, green infrastructure investment, and support for green entrepreneurship. A well-designed policy framework can create a supportive environment for businesses to grow while simultaneously creating job opportunities for workers.

Governments can incentivize the creation of green jobs through subsidies for renewable energy projects, tax credits for clean energy companies, and investment in public infrastructure that supports green technologies, such as electric vehicle charging stations and smart grids. In countries like Germany, Denmark, and China, government support has been instrumental in driving the renewable energy transition, providing a model for other nations to follow.

On the private side, companies across various industries—construction, manufacturing, transportation, and agriculture—are increasingly embracing sustainability practices and recognizing the value of green innovation. Whether it's through the development of new green technologies, the adoption of clean energy solutions, or the creation of sustainable supply chains, businesses that prioritize environmental responsibility are driving the demand for green jobs and reshaping the global workforce.

The private sector, particularly large corporations, has a pivotal role to play in both fostering and expanding green job opportunities. By prioritizing sustainability in their business models, corporations can create demand for green jobs in supply chain management, sustainability consulting, carbon accounting, and other related fields. However, this must be accompanied by a genuine commitment to environmental responsibility rather than just greenwashing.

4. The Importance of Green Jobs in Communities

Green jobs not only address environmental concerns but also offer a powerful tool for community development, particularly in regions facing economic hardship due to the decline of traditional industries like coal, steel, and manufacturing. In many rural areas, small towns, and post-industrial communities, green jobs can serve as a path to economic revitalization. For example, a small town that once relied on coal mining could transition to solar panel manufacturing or wind farm installation, creating jobs for local residents while contributing to the fight against climate change.

Investing in green job creation in low-income communities and communities of color is particularly critical. These communities are often the hardest hit by environmental degradation, experiencing the disproportionate impacts of pollution, climate change, and ecosystem loss. By creating green job opportunities in these areas, governments and businesses can contribute to environmental justice while lifting people out of poverty and creating pathways to upward mobility.

The need for green jobs is more urgent than ever. As the world faces unprecedented environmental challenges, the demand for workers in clean energy, sustainable agriculture, environmental restoration, and green manufacturing is skyrocketing. Green jobs offer a unique opportunity to transition away from harmful industries, create new economic opportunities, and address climate change while contributing to social equity and environmental justice. However, to unlock this potential, we must invest in education, training, and infrastructure to ensure that workers are equipped with the skills necessary for a sustainable, green economy.

The creation of green jobs is not just about environmental sustainability—it is about rebuilding economies, reducing inequality, and ensuring that the next generation of workers has the tools and opportunities to thrive in a rapidly changing world. The future of work is green, and we must act now to ensure that workers are ready to meet the challenges and opportunities that lie ahead.

Retraining Workers Displaced by Technology

As the global economy rapidly transitions toward a more sustainable future, one of the most significant challenges we face is the displacement of workers from industries that are being phased out due to technological advancements, automation, and the urgent need to combat climate change. The fossil fuel industry, traditional manufacturing sectors, and even agriculture are undergoing profound transformations, often rendering entire categories of jobs obsolete or significantly reduced. To ensure a just transition for these workers, we must prioritize retraining and reskilling initiatives that empower displaced individuals to thrive in the green economy.

The reality is that while new jobs are emerging in renewable energy, sustainable agriculture, and environmental protection, these roles often require different skills than those possessed by workers in industries like coal mining, oil drilling, or traditional car manufacturing. Without targeted retraining and education programs, many workers risk being left behind, perpetuating economic inequality and exacerbating social divides. The transition to a green economy must be inclusive, providing pathways for workers of all ages and backgrounds to acquire the skills they need to participate in a sustainable, high-tech, low-carbon world.

1. Understanding the Scope of Technological Displacement

Technological advancements—particularly in automation, artificial intelligence, and renewable energy technologies—are rapidly reshaping labor markets. According to the World Economic Forum, automation and artificial intelligence (AI) could displace 85 million jobs worldwide by 2025, particularly in fields that involve routine, manual, or low-skilled labor. In sectors like coal mining, oil extraction, and automotive manufacturing, automation is already replacing jobs at an alarming rate. For example, self-driving trucks are expected to eliminate hundreds of thousands of driving jobs, while advancements in robotics and automated drilling threaten to displace workers in oil and gas extraction.

This wave of job displacement presents a profound challenge, particularly in regions where fossil fuel-based industries are a primary source of employment. In the United States, for example, thousands of workers in coal and natural gas extraction have already lost their jobs due to the rise of renewable energy sources like solar and wind, which require far fewer workers to operate. Similarly, traditional car manufacturing jobs are at risk due to the shift towards electric vehicles (EVs), which require different manufacturing processes and fewer components than conventional internal combustion engine vehicles.

While these technological advancements offer tremendous benefits in terms of efficiency and environmental sustainability, they also create a labor market disconnect, with workers in declining industries needing to pivot to new sectors. Unfortunately, this pivot is not always easy. Workers in traditional sectors often lack the specific skills required to work in clean energy, green building, or sustainable agriculture, creating a barrier to entry for those looking to transition to the green economy.

2. The Need for Proactive Retraining Programs

The best way to address these challenges is through proactive retraining programs that prepare displaced workers for the jobs of the future. Governments, educational institutions, and employers must work together to create targeted reskilling initiatives that offer both technical expertise and soft skills—all tailored to the demands of the green economy.

Government Support and Public Policy:

Governments play a crucial role in facilitating this transition. Public policy should include investments in job retraining programs, vocational education, and apprenticeships in sustainable industries. For instance, countries like Germany and Denmark have long recognized the need for retraining programs in response to the decline of traditional industries and the rise of renewable energy. Germany's Energy Transition or Energiewende initiative, for example, has not only shifted the country's energy landscape toward renewables but also invested heavily in retraining workers from fossil fuel sectors to ensure that they can transition to green jobs in wind and solar industries.

A strong public policy framework should include:

- **Government subsidies** for retraining programs that focus on high-demand green industries such as **solar energy, wind power, battery technology**, and **sustainable agriculture**.
- **Education partnerships** between universities, technical colleges, and vocational schools to develop curricula that provide the skills needed for the green economy.
- **Retraining grants** and **tax incentives** for companies that invest in reskilling their workforce.
- **Worker transition plans** that provide financial assistance, job counseling, and mentorship for displaced workers as they navigate their career changes.

By investing in these programs, governments can ensure that workers displaced by technological disruption aren't left behind in the old economy but instead become integral contributors to the green transformation.

Employer Responsibility:

Employers, particularly in industries that are introducing automation or adopting cleaner technologies, must also shoulder some of the responsibility for retraining workers. In fact, companies that invest in retraining their employees benefit in the long term by retaining skilled labor, improving worker loyalty, and contributing to their community's economic stability. For example, solar companies or wind energy manufacturers could partner with community colleges to offer on-the-job training and certification programs, helping workers transition smoothly into these growing sectors.

In the automotive industry, major manufacturers such as Ford, General Motors, and Tesla are already shifting their focus to electric vehicles, which require new manufacturing processes, technology integration, and specialized skills. These companies should prioritize training programs for workers transitioning from internal combustion engine (ICE) vehicle production to EVs. Similarly, automakers can invest in upskilling programs that teach workers new skills in battery technology, electric motor assembly, and vehicle software to ensure that no worker is left behind in the transformation of the sector.

Corporate-led retraining efforts could be supported by initiatives such as:

- **Internal career transition programs** that offer employees the chance to gain new skills while remaining with the company.
- **Partnerships with technical schools and universities** to develop customized courses for industries undergoing significant change.
- **Mentorship and apprenticeship programs** that help displaced workers learn new trades from experienced professionals in emerging sectors.

Education and Training Institutions:

Higher education institutions, especially community colleges and technical schools, are at the forefront of training displaced workers for the green economy. In particular, these institutions can offer short-term certification programs that allow workers to acquire new, marketable skills without the time or financial commitment required for a full degree.

Community colleges are well-positioned to provide localized, affordable training in key areas such as:

- **Renewable energy technologies** (solar, wind, geothermal, hydropower)
- **Energy-efficient building design** and **green construction practices**
- **Sustainable agriculture techniques** like **permaculture, regenerative farming, and vertical farming**

- **Battery storage** and **electric vehicle maintenance**
- **Waste management and recycling**

These institutions should work closely with industry leaders to ensure that their curricula match the specific skills required in green sectors. By building strong relationships with employers and ensuring that training programs are market-driven, educational institutions can help workers gain the skills that employers are actively seeking.

3. A Lifelong Learning Model

The retraining effort should not be a one-time event but a lifelong learning model. As technology continues to evolve, the workforce needs to be flexible and adaptive to new industries and job roles. By embedding continuous education into career paths, workers can stay ahead of technological disruptions and take advantage of emerging opportunities.

This lifelong learning model could be supported by:

- **Online learning platforms** that provide accessible, low-cost training in new technologies.
- **Partnerships between the public and private sectors** to provide workers with access to ongoing **job skills upgrading**.
- **Employee-driven learning initiatives** that allow workers to access professional development opportunities at every stage of their careers.

Retraining workers displaced by technology is a vital step toward building a green economy that works for everyone. While the transition to renewable energy, automation, and other technologies presents challenges, it also offers an opportunity to provide dignified, sustainable work in the sectors of the future. Through robust government policies, employer investment in reskilling programs, and targeted educational opportunities, we can help displaced workers find new paths in green industries. By ensuring that workers are equipped with the right skills and resources, we can create an economy that is not only environmentally sustainable but also economically inclusive. This shift will empower workers, safeguard jobs, and provide a blueprint for the world's transition to a cleaner, greener, and more just future.

Successful Job Creation Examples

The need for green jobs is clear, but what makes this transition more hopeful is the growing number of real-world examples where sustainable job creation is not only possible but already happening. Across the globe, countries, regions, and companies are developing innovative strategies to create jobs that serve both the environment and the economy. These examples not only showcase the potential of a green workforce but also offer valuable lessons in how to ensure that future job creation is equitable, scalable, and sustainable.

1. The Green New Deal in the United States

One of the most ambitious examples of job creation through environmental policies is the Green New Deal (GND) proposal in the United States. Although it has not yet been fully implemented, the GND is a bold vision for transforming the American economy by addressing climate change while ensuring economic justice. By investing in renewable energy, energy efficiency, sustainable infrastructure, and green manufacturing, the GND aims to create millions of new jobsin industries such as solar, wind, electric vehicles, and green construction.

According to various studies, such as those conducted by the Union of Concerned Scientists, transitioning to a clean energy economy could create up to 25 million jobs in the U.S. by 2030. These jobs would span a broad range of sectors—from solar panel installers and wind turbine technicians to energy auditors and green architects. The GND is a critical example of how comprehensive policy proposals can serve as blueprints for mass job creation in the green economy, especially when combined with robust worker training programs and union protections.

2. Germany's Energiewende and the Renewable Energy Boom

Germany's Energiewende (Energy Transition) is one of the most successful examples of how government policy can catalyze the growth of green jobs at a national level. This ambitious program, launched in 2010, aims to transition the country away from nuclear energy and fossil fuels while drastically reducing carbon emissions. As part of this strategy, Germany has invested heavily in renewable energy, including wind, solar, and bioenergy, and has successfully transformed its energy sector.

Between 2004 and 2019, the renewable energy sector in Germany grew from 150,000 jobs to more than 300,000—a staggering growth rate. Key contributors to this job creation include the manufacturing and installation of solar panels, the construction of wind turbines, and the development of energy storage systems. One of the standout success stories within the Energiewende framework is Germany's wind energy sector, which alone employs more than 100,000 workers and is one of the largest wind turbine manufacturers in the world.

Moreover, Germany's approach to integrating worker retraining programs into the renewable energy transition has set a standard for other countries to follow. Through public-private partnerships and collaboration with vocational schools, Germany has ensured that displaced workers from fossil fuel industries have opportunities to learn new skills in clean energy fields, paving the way for a just transition.

3. The Rise of Solar Jobs in India

India, as one of the world's fastest-growing economies and largest greenhouse gas emitters, has also been at the forefront of green job creation, particularly in the solar energy sector.

In recent years, India has committed to scaling up its renewable energy capacity, with an ambitious target of 100 gigawatts (GW) of solar power by 2022. The Indian government has used this target to drive the creation of thousands of jobs in solar energy, particularly in solar panel manufacturing, installation, and maintenance.

A notable success story comes from Gujarat, one of the country's leading solar hubs. The state's government invested in large-scale solar parks, which helped create thousands of jobs in the region, particularly for migrant workers, women, and low-income communities. In 2020, India's solar industry alone employed more than 1 million people, and the Indian Solar Manufacturers Association estimates that this could grow to 3 million by 2030.

India's solar success also highlights how inclusive job creation can help tackle poverty while contributing to global climate goals. The country's initiatives, like training programs for women in solar installation and local job creation in rural areas, have shown that green jobs can be a pathway to economic empowerment for marginalized communities, providing stable incomes and improving local living standards.

4. Job Creation in Electric Vehicle Manufacturing (China)

China, the world's largest emitter of greenhouse gases, has also made significant strides in creating green jobs, particularly in the burgeoning electric vehicle (EV) sector. Over the last decade, China has become a global leader in electric vehicle production, and with this growth, millions of new jobs have been created in manufacturing, research and development, and EV infrastructure. The China New Energy Vehicle (NEV) program, which aims to have 20% of all vehicles in the country be electric by 2025, has incentivized the growth of the EV industry, providing new opportunities for both skilled labor and technicians.

In cities like Shenzhen, home to the world's largest fleet of electric buses, thousands of workers have found jobs in EV manufacturing, battery production, and charging station installation. Companies like BYD, NIO, and Geely are leading the charge in electric vehicle innovation, employing hundreds of thousands of workers in China. The rise of the EV supply chain, including battery producers and component manufacturers, is driving job creation in regions previously dependent on traditional automotive industries, such as automobile parts suppliers and gasoline vehicle production plants.

This shift to electric vehicles has created a new, rapidly expanding sector that offers opportunities for workers to transition from fossil fuel-dependent jobs to those that support the transition to a clean, sustainable future. The EV industry's global supply chain, from raw material extraction to vehicle assembly and vehicle maintenance, is a shining example of how green jobs can drive industrial revitalization and economic growth.

5. Local Job Creation Through Sustainable Agriculture (United States)

In the United States, sustainable agriculture is becoming a driving force in job creation, particularly in regions that have experienced economic decline due to industrial farming practices. The rise of organic farming, regenerative agriculture, and local food systems has created thousands of new positions, from farmers and ranchers to agriculture technicians and supply chain managers.

One compelling example comes from California, where the Regenerative Agriculture Alliance has worked to transition traditional farms to more sustainable practices that prioritize soil health, water conservation, and biodiversity. These practices have resulted in a resurgence of family-owned farms, providing new job opportunities in rural communities that are often struggling with high levels of unemployment and poverty. Additionally, programs like Farm to School and urban farming initiatives are creating local jobs that support food security, improve nutrition, and build stronger local economies.

The examples above show that creating green jobs is not just a theoretical goal—it is happening right now across the globe. From Germany's energy transition to India's solar boom and China's electric vehicle revolution, the growth of green industries is proving that sustainable job creation is not only possible but can also be economically transformative. Whether through large-scale government policies or small community-driven initiatives, the green economy offers vast potential for creating high-quality, stable jobs that benefit both the environment and society.

These success stories highlight that green job creation is not a pipe dream but a practical reality that can provide economic opportunities for communities around the world—especially those most impacted by economic inequality and environmental degradation. For a truly just and sustainable transition, governments, businesses, and educational institutions must continue to invest in training, education, and worker support programs to ensure that no one is left behind. By doing so, we can build a global economy that is both green and inclusive, creating a sustainable future for all.

Chapter 9

Legislation for a Sustainable Future

Governments play a crucial role in shaping the future of our planet, not only through their regulation of industries and environmental protections but also by leading the way in creating policies that drive sustainability, innovation, and equity. As the world faces increasingly severe environmental crises, from climate change to biodiversity loss, governments must act with urgency and purpose to create and enforce policies that protect the environment and pave the way for a greener economy. The role of government is multifaceted, extending far beyond creating laws and regulations; it involves fostering collaboration, investing in green technologies, and ensuring a just transition for workers and communities most affected by environmental changes.

1. The Role of Government in Setting Environmental Standards

A government's primary responsibility is to establish laws and regulations that define the rules of the game for industries, companies, and citizens. Environmental laws—such as carbon emission standards, water pollution regulations, and protected area designations—set the framework for how businesses and individuals must interact with natural resources, and they are key to ensuring that environmental damage is mitigated and the public good is safeguarded.

For example, in the United States, landmark environmental regulations like the Clean Air Act (1970), the Clean Water Act (1972), and the Endangered Species Act (1973) have been instrumental in reducing air and water pollution, protecting critical wildlife habitats, and reducing threats to biodiversity. These laws have not only helped improve the quality of life for millions of people but have also been pivotal in holding polluting industries accountable.

But the government's role in environmental policy goes beyond simply regulating pollution and managing natural resources. It involves setting ambitious climate targets, incentivizing green technologies, and encouraging sustainable development. This is critical because without the government's authority to legislate and enforce environmental protection, the massive power of large corporations would undermine any genuine attempt to address the crises we face.

Governments must use their power to:

- **Set clear, enforceable emissions standards** for industries, particularly for fossil fuel extraction and manufacturing.
- **Incentivize clean energy production** by offering tax credits or grants to companies developing wind, solar, and other renewable technologies.
- **Hold polluting industries accountable**, by imposing penalties and sanctions for non-compliance with environmental laws.
- **Create policies that protect biodiversity**, by establishing and enforcing protected areas for wildlife, and investing in **habitat restoration** programs.

2. Leading Climate Action with Ambitious Targets

One of the most important roles of government in the context of environmental policy is to set and commit to ambitious climate targets. These targets send a strong signal to industries, investors, and the public that action on climate change is both urgent and necessary. Governments must take the lead in establishing science-based emissions reduction targets and committing to international agreements that hold countries accountable for their contributions to climate action.

For example, the Paris Agreement (2015) is a landmark global accord that saw nearly 200 countries come together with the common goal of limiting global warming to well below 2°C, and ideally 1.5°C, above pre-industrial levels. Under the Paris Agreement, each nation is expected to set nationally determined contributions (NDCs)—quantifiable emissions reduction targets—and take meaningful steps toward achieving them.

The responsibility of government doesn't end with signing such agreements. In fact, domestic policy plays a critical role in meeting the targets set in international accords. For instance, carbon pricing mechanisms such as carbon taxes or cap-and-trade systems can be implemented by national governments to ensure that the true environmental cost of emissions is accounted for in market transactions. Governments can also incentivize the transition to cleaner energy by offering subsidies for renewable energy sources, while gradually eliminating subsidies for fossil fuels.

Countries like Denmark, Norway, and Costa Rica have been pioneers in setting ambitious renewable energy goals and have demonstrated that policy can drive large-scale transformation in the energy sector. Denmark aims to be carbon-neutral by 2050, while Costa Rica is already achieving remarkable success with 100% renewable energy generation for much of its electricity needs. These countries are not only reducing their carbon footprints but are also reaping the economic and social benefits of these sustainable policies, including job creation, energy security, and a more resilient economy.

3. Incentivizing Green Innovation and Technologies

Governments are also pivotal in driving green innovation by creating a policy environment that encourages the development and scaling of clean technologies. This can be done through research and development (R&D) funding, tax incentives, and public-private partnerships aimed at fostering the growth of emerging industries such as clean energy, electric vehicles, carbon capture, and sustainable agriculture.

Governments can also invest directly in infrastructure that supports a green economy, such as:

- **Electric vehicle charging networks** and **public transit systems** powered by renewable energy.
- **Smart grids** that improve the efficiency and distribution of renewable energy.
- **Sustainable agriculture practices** through subsidies for regenerative farming or **urban farming initiatives**.

In addition to fostering innovation through financial support, governments can create market demand for clean technologies by passing laws that prioritize the use of green products and services. For instance, the California Clean Car Standards set vehicle efficiency standards that far exceeded federal requirements, driving innovation in the automotive industry and accelerating the development of electric vehicles (EVs). Similarly, green building standards(e.g., LEED certification) encourage the construction of energy-efficient homes and commercial buildings, spurring demand for sustainable building materials and technologies.

Governments can also encourage private sector investment in green technologies by ensuring that there are clear and supportive policies in place. The US Investment Tax Credit for solar energy, for example, has been instrumental in stimulating the growth of the solar industry by reducing the upfront cost of solar systems and making them more attractive for residential and commercial installations. Carbon capture and storage (CCS) technologies also receive government incentives for pilot projects, bringing innovative solutions to market that could be key to reaching net-zero emissions.

4. Ensuring a Just Transition for Workers and Communities

As industries transition to more sustainable practices, the government must play a central role in ensuring that the economic benefits of green policies are shared equitably and that no community is left behind. This is particularly important for workers and regions that depend on high-carbon industries such as coal, oil, and gas. The shift to a green economy presents a significant challenge for workers who may face job displacement due to the closure of polluting industries, but it also offers a unique opportunity to retrain workers for the green sectors of the future.

Governments must ensure that the transition to a low-carbon economy is fair and inclusive. This can be achieved through:

- Retraining programs that provide workers with new skills in renewable energy, sustainable agriculture, and clean manufacturing.
- Economic diversification efforts to create jobs in green sectors for regions dependent on fossil fuel extraction and other carbon-intensive industries.
- Community investment programs to support areas that are economically vulnerable to the transition, such as former coal mining towns or regions heavily reliant on the oil and gas sector.

Countries like Canada and the United Kingdom have implemented Just Transition Plans, which outline specific measures to support affected workers and communities. These plans often include financial support, retraining programs, and infrastructure investment to help workers shift to new jobs in clean industries. Such policies can ensure that environmental policies are both socially just and economically resilient, fostering a green economy that benefits all citizens.

The government's role in shaping environmental policies cannot be overstated. From setting emissions standards to fostering green innovation, supporting renewable energy development, and ensuring a just transition for workers, governments must act decisively and with foresight. By creating a policy landscape that is supportive of sustainability, governments can drive the transformation necessary to protect the planet, create millions of new jobs, and ensure a more equitable and resilient future for all. Without strong governmental action, the environmental challenges we face will remain unaddressed, and the potential for a truly green economy will continue to slip away.

Case Studies of Blocked Legislation

While the need for comprehensive environmental legislation is universally recognized, there are countless instances where meaningful bills designed to protect our planet have been either blocked, watered down, or delayed due to corporate influence and political resistance. This resistance often stems from industries with a vested interest in maintaining the status quo—whether it's the fossil fuel sector, agricultural giants, or multinational corporations that profit from environmentally destructive practices. Understanding these case studies is crucial, as they not only highlight the power of corporate lobbying but also underscore the need for a political will that prioritizes environmental action over economic short-term gains.

1. The Green New Deal: A Vision Denied

In the United States, one of the most ambitious pieces of environmental legislation to gain significant attention in recent years is the Green New Deal (GND). Proposed in 2019 by Congresswoman Alexandria Ocasio-Cortez and Senator Ed Markey, the Green New Deal called for sweeping investments in clean energy, decarbonization of industries, universal healthcare, affordable housing, and job creation in the green economy. The idea was simple but radical: to address the interconnected crises of climate change, inequality, and economic stagnation, all while creating millions of sustainable jobs. The GND was seen as a potential blueprint for the future of climate action—a comprehensive solution to the most pressing issues of the 21st century.

However, the proposal faced fierce opposition from several sectors, including the fossil fuel industry, right-wing political groups, and corporate lobbyists. Industry-funded political action committees (PACs) and conservative think tanks launched an all-out campaign against the GND, framing it as an unrealistic, economy-destroying "socialist" agenda. In March 2019, a Senate vote on the Green New Deal ended in a stunning defeat, with 57 senators voting against it, and only 43 voting in favor. The measure didn't even receive enough support from moderate Democrats, many of whom were swayed by the political and economic power of the fossil fuel sector.

The failure of the Green New Deal illustrates the stark political divide on climate action, where the influence of fossil fuel giants like ExxonMobil, Chevron, and BP can significantly impact policymaking. These companies, along with their allies in the Senate and House of Representatives, have spent millions in lobbying efforts to weaken climate legislation and promote their continued profitability. This resistance has successfully blocked any real shift toward comprehensive climate action, with even moderate proposals often stalled or undermined.

2. The Clean Power Plan: A Victory for the Coal Industry

Another striking example of blocked climate legislation is the Clean Power Plan (CPP), introduced during the Obama administration in 2015. The CPP aimed to reduce carbon emissions from power plants by setting state-specific targets for carbon reduction, encouraging the use of renewable energy, and promoting energy efficiency. It was hailed as one of the most significant efforts in U.S. history to curb greenhouse gas emissions from the country's largest source of pollution—coal-fired power plants.

However, the plan faced intense opposition from the coal industry, which saw it as a direct threat to its long-standing dominance in the energy sector. Coal companies such as Peabody Energy, Arch Coal, and Alpha Natural Resources lobbied heavily against the CPP, spending millions of dollars in campaign contributions to key politicians who would oppose it. In 2016, the Supreme Court of the United States issued a stay on the plan, temporarily halting its implementation. Despite being backed by the Environmental Protection Agency (EPA) and environmental advocates, the CPP was eventually repealed by the Trump administration in 2019, in part due to lobbying from the fossil fuel industry and Republican lawmakers sympathetic to their cause.

The defeat of the Clean Power Plan is a case study in how well-funded interest groups can obstruct progressive environmental policies. The coal industry's influence on the American political system has been so profound that even policies intended to mitigate climate change are routinely blocked in favor of industry interests. This example also underscores the role of judicial and legislative branches in thwarting executive actions, even those that have widespread public support.

3. The Paris Agreement: A Struggle for Commitment

One of the most significant global environmental agreements in recent history is the Paris Agreement, adopted in 2015 at the UN Climate Change Conference (COP21). The Paris Agreement seeks to limit global temperature rise to well below 2°C, with a focus on reducing global carbon emissions to net-zero by 2050. While the agreement was hailed as a historic achievement and brought together nearly 200 countries, the path to full implementation has been fraught with difficulties—chief among them being the withdrawal of the United States under the Trump administration.

In 2017, President Donald Trump announced that the U.S. would be pulling out of the Paris Agreement, citing concerns about economic consequences and the agreement's potential to harm American businesses. The decision to withdraw was largely influenced by lobbying from industries such as coal, oil, and natural gas, which feared stricter regulations and emission reduction targets. Despite the scientific consensus on the urgent need for global action on climate change, powerful political and corporate interests managed to undermine the U.S.'s role in global climate leadership.

Although the United States rejoined the Paris Agreement under President Joe Biden in 2021, the episode highlights the vulnerability of international climate agreements to national political dynamics and the undue influence of corporations with a vested interest in maintaining fossil fuel dominance. In this case, corporate lobbying played a decisive role in delaying collective action on climate change and eroding trust in international commitments.

4. The Biodiversity Crisis: Defunding the Convention on Biological Diversity

While much of the global climate discussion focuses on carbon emissions and climate change, there is another environmental crisis that has largely been ignored by lawmakers: the loss of biodiversity. Efforts to create and implement policies to address biodiversity loss have been stymied by corporations involved in deforestation, industrial agriculture, and wildlife trafficking.

In 2020, a UN biodiversity summit was scheduled to discuss the post-2020 global biodiversity framework, a set of ambitious targets aimed at reversing biodiversity loss by 2030. However, efforts to increase funding for conservation efforts and biodiversity protection have faced consistent resistance. Agribusiness giants, like Cargill and ADM, which are heavily involved in deforestation and land-grabbing, have lobbied governments to dilute commitments to halt forest destruction and prioritize business interests over biodiversity protection. These lobbying efforts were evident during the Convention on Biological Diversity (CBD) negotiations, where financial commitments to biodiversity conservation were severely reduced due to pressure from multinational agricultural corporations.

The resistance to global biodiversity agreements demonstrates how corporate interests that profit from environmental degradation can disrupt or block meaningful international efforts to protect the planet's ecosystems. Without binding policies that incentivize conservation, it is unlikely that governments will meet their biodiversity targets, undermining the long-term health of ecosystems, species, and communities that depend on them.

5. The Endangered Species Act: A Political Battleground

In the United States, the Endangered Species Act (ESA), passed in 1973, has been one of the most important laws for protecting biodiversity, preventing the extinction of species, and preserving their habitats. However, this critical piece of legislation has been a target of political lobbying by industry groups, especially those involved in logging, mining, and oil extraction. In recent years, the law has faced serious attempts to weaken its provisions, particularly regarding the listing of endangered species and the protection of critical habitats.

For example, in 2018, the Trump administration proposed changes to the ESA that would limit the criteria for listing species as endangered, thus protecting businesses from having to alter projects or activities that would threaten endangered species' habitats. Lobbying by the National Association of Home Builders (NAHB) and other pro-business groups led to these proposed changes. They argued that such protections were harming economic development. Environmental groups, however, warned that weakening the ESA would result in further loss of biodiversity and irreparable damage to ecosystems.

Despite public outcry and opposition from environmental advocates, many of these proposed changes were pushed through, demonstrating how corporate interests can successfully influence legislation meant to protect wildlife and ecosystems.

These case studies of blocked or weakened environmental legislation highlight the immense challenge that governments face when attempting to enact meaningful reforms. Whether it is the Green New Deal, the Clean Power Plan, or global agreements like the Paris Accord, the force of corporate lobbying and political resistance from vested interests is a major barrier to climate action. In each of these cases, powerful industries have used their financial and political leverage to block policies that would create long-term environmental benefits, often at the expense of public health, biodiversity, and climate stability.

Ultimately, these examples underscore the need for governments to overcome these barriers and pass stronger, more effective environmental legislation—no matter how much pressure is exerted by industries seeking to preserve the status quo. Public support for robust climate action is high, and it is imperative that leaders in government and business work together to ensure the future of our planet is not compromised by corporate interests.

International Cooperation

Environmental challenges do not respect borders. Climate change, biodiversity loss, ocean pollution, and resource depletion are global issues that require global solutions. While national policies are essential for domestic progress, true environmental sustainability can only be achieved through international cooperation. The scale and complexity of the crises demand a united effort, where countries collaborate, share resources and knowledge, and hold each other accountable for meeting global targets.

The Paris Agreement: A Global Framework

One of the most significant examples of international cooperation on climate change is the Paris Agreement—a legally binding international treaty adopted in 2015 under the United Nations Framework Convention on Climate Change (UNFCCC). The agreement's central goal is to limit global temperature rise to well below 2°C, with efforts to limit it to 1.5°C compared to pre-industrial levels. Almost every country on the planet, including major emitters like the United States, China, and the European Union, has committed to reducing greenhouse gas emissions, investing in clean energy, and enhancing their climate resilience.

However, despite the agreement's widespread acceptance, challenges remain in terms of financial commitments, transparency, and enforcement. Many nations, particularly developing countries, argue that they are being asked to shoulder a disproportionate burden without sufficient financial and technological support. Conversely, developed nations have been reluctant to commit the funds necessary to help poorer nations transition to cleaner energy and adapt to the impacts of climate change.

The role of corporate interests cannot be overlooked in this context, either. Some countries, particularly those with heavy investments in fossil fuels or deforestation, have lobbied to weaken their climate targets. For example, Brazil's government, under former President Jair Bolsonaro, faced international criticism for weakening its commitments to protect the Amazon rainforest, one of the world's most critical carbon sinks. Similarly, Australia faced global scrutiny for its continued reliance on coal and gas, despite its pledges to reduce emissions under the Paris Agreement.

The Paris Agreement demonstrates that international cooperation is vital but also fraught with complexities. While the accord has created a common platform for action, inconsistent enforcement, and lobbying from fossil fuel industries continue to hinder its effectiveness. To ensure success, countries must go beyond rhetoric and make meaningful changes— driving global collaboration, ensuring financial equity, and holding each other accountable.

Global Biodiversity Agreements

Another critical area of international cooperation is biodiversity conservation. Biodiversity loss, particularly the destruction of ecosystems like forests and coral reefs, is a threat that crosses borders. Yet, unlike climate change, which has clear global indicators like rising temperatures and atmospheric CO2 levels, the loss of biodiversity is harder to measure on a global scale. Nevertheless, several important international agreements have been forged to tackle this issue.

The Convention on Biological Diversity (CBD), which was adopted in 1992, is an international treaty aimed at conserving biodiversity, promoting its sustainable use, and ensuring the fair sharing of benefits derived from genetic resources. In 2020, the UN Biodiversity Conference (COP15), held virtually, set a target to protect 30% of the world's land and oceans by 2030—a vital step in halting species extinction and preserving ecosystems.

However, global cooperation on biodiversity faces significant obstacles. For one, the financial commitments made by wealthier nations to help developing countries conserve biodiversity are often insufficient. The 2021 Global Biodiversity Outlook found that while many countries are pledging ambitious conservation targets, the funding shortfalls remain a critical bottleneck. Moreover, powerful industries such as logging, mining, and agriculture continue to exert political pressure to undermine regulations that protect ecosystems.

One glaring example is the Amazon rainforest—a critical global resource that provides ecosystem services for millions of people. While countries like Brazil and Peru are signatories to international biodiversity agreements, the rapid deforestation driven by illegal logging, agribusiness, and mining often goes unchecked. International cooperation on biodiversity must address global supply chains, from palm oil production to soy farming, and include stricter regulations on multinational companies involved in biodiversity loss.

The Role of Multinational Corporations and Supply Chains

To truly tackle global environmental issues, international cooperation must go beyond government agreements. Multinational corporations, which often span multiple countries, have an outsized impact on the environment, particularly in sectors such as oil extraction, agriculture, and manufacturing. These companies' supply chains, often spread across the globe, influence environmental policy and regulations in the countries where they operate.

The EU's 2020 Green Deal, for example, emphasizes a green recovery from the COVID-19 pandemic and aims to position Europe as a leader in global sustainable development. It focuses on sustainable supply chains, carbon border taxes, and investment in green infrastructure. However, for the EU's Green Deal—and similar international frameworks to succeed—corporate accountability must be at the forefront. Multinational companies must be held accountable for their environmental footprint, regardless of where they operate.

International cooperation in regulating global corporations is essential in the fight against climate change and biodiversity loss. Regulatory frameworks that address cross-border pollution, deforestation, and resource extraction must be created and enforced globally. International organizations like the United Nations Environment Programme (UNEP)and the World Trade Organization (WTO) must take a more prominent role in enforcing corporate responsibility and ensuring that environmental standards are maintained across international borders.

The Road Ahead for Global Cooperation

As climate change and environmental degradation continue to escalate, the call for international cooperation has never been more urgent. The Paris Agreement, the CBD, and other global frameworks provide a critical starting point, but countries must go further to strengthen enforcement mechanisms, ensure adequate financial support for developing nations, and push for real corporate accountability. Without a truly global effort—one that integrates government action, corporate responsibility, and public support—the world risks falling short of its environmental goals.

In this chapter, we have seen the significant role legislation plays in addressing environmental issues. While corporate lobbying and political resistance have often blocked or diluted meaningful environmental legislation, international cooperation provides a path forward. The case studies highlighted here—whether the Green New Deal, the Clean Power Plan, or global agreements like the Paris Agreement—demonstrate the profound challenges we face.

Yet, these challenges are not insurmountable. Governments must take a stand against corporate interests that undermine environmental progress, while at the same time fostering international cooperation and enforcing global agreements. Corporations, too, must be held accountable for their role in the degradation of the planet and held to higher standards of sustainability. Only through concerted action—at the local, national, and global levels— can we hope to secure a sustainable future for generations to come.

The need for bold legislative action, robust global frameworks, and the collective commitment of governments, corporations, and individuals has never been greater. We must act now to ensure that the planet we leave behind is one that future generations can inherit, not one that is irreparably damaged by short-sightedness and greed.

Chapter 10

The Power of Individuals and Communities
How We Can All Make a Difference

While large-scale policy changes, corporate accountability, and international agreements are essential to addressing the environmental crises we face, individual action is just as crucial. Often, it feels like the responsibility for solving environmental problems rests with governments or corporations, leaving people feeling helpless or insignificant in the fight against climate change and other ecological challenges. However, the truth is that each of us has the power to make a significant impact on the planet's health—both through our daily choices and by inspiring collective action.

The Ripple Effect of Personal Choices

Every action we take—no matter how small—ripples outward, creating a larger effect. The choices we make in our consumer habits, energy use, waste disposal, and transportation can contribute to a greener future or perpetuate the very systems that harm the planet. When we choose to buy sustainably, conserve energy, reduce waste, and support environmentally conscious businesses, we send a clear message to the market: sustainability matters. As demand for green products, services, and practices rises, companies are incentivized to innovate and shift their business models to align with consumer values.

For instance, the rise of the plant-based food industry—driven in part by growing consumer interest in reducing animal agriculture's environmental footprint—has prompted fast food chains and supermarkets to expand their vegan and vegetarian options. This shift is helping reduce greenhouse gas emissions, deforestation, and water usage associated with meat production. Similarly, the surge in demand for renewable energy options—like rooftop solar panels and electric vehicles—has spurred major companies to invest in cleaner alternatives to fossil fuels.

Conscious Consumerism: Voting with Your Wallet

One of the most powerful tools at an individual's disposal is their wallet. What we choose to buy, invest in, and support financially can drastically shape the demand for sustainable products and eco-friendly services. In fact, the concept of conscious consumerism—making purchasing decisions based on environmental impact—is one of the most effective ways to accelerate systemic change.

For example, individuals can make a significant impact by choosing products that are ethically sourced, fair-trade certified, and environmentally friendly. Opting for items that are made with recycled materials, have minimal packaging, or support local economies reduces the environmental burden of production, transportation, and waste. By supporting companies that prioritize sustainable sourcing, low-carbon manufacturing, and recyclable packaging, consumers signal to the market that sustainability is a priority.

Additionally, corporate transparency is becoming more of a demand than a desire, as consumers increasingly seek brands that are open about their environmental and social impact. Companies that practice greenwashing—pretending to be sustainable without making meaningful changes—are being called out by activists, journalists, and consumers alike. This growing scrutiny means that businesses can no longer afford to simply pay lip service to sustainability without making actual changes. Consumers have the power to **reward responsible companies** and **penalize those that refuse to change**.

Minimizing Your Carbon Footprint

A key element of empowering personal action is reducing your carbon footprint. This involves making intentional choices that lower your personal contribution to climate change. A carbon footprint refers to the total greenhouse gases emitted as a result of human activities, especially those associated with energy use, food production, transportation, and waste generation.

Here are a few impactful actions individuals can take to reduce their carbon footprint:

1. **Energy Efficiency**: Switch to LED lightbulbs, upgrade to energy-efficient appliances, and seal windows and doors to minimize heating and cooling costs. If possible, install a solar panel system or consider green energy options through your local utility provider.

2. **Transportation Choices**: Reducing car travel is one of the most effective ways to cut your carbon emissions. Consider walking, biking, using public transportation, or carpooling. If you must drive, choose a fuel-efficient car or opt for an electric vehicle (EV) to cut down on fuel consumption and emissions.

3. **Food Choices**: The food we eat has a significant environmental footprint, particularly when it comes to meat production. Shifting towards a more plant-based diet—even reducing meat consumption to a few days a week—can reduce emissions, water usage, and land degradation. Buying local and seasonal produce also helps lower the environmental costs of transportation and storage.

4. **Waste Reduction: Reducing, reusing, and recycling** are simple but effective strategies for minimizing waste. Composting food scraps, avoiding single-use plastics, and purchasing items in bulk can help cut down on the amount of trash that ends up in landfills and oceans.

5.   **Water Conservation**: Use water wisely by fixing leaky faucets, taking shorter showers, and using water-efficient appliances. In areas where water is scarce, being conscious of water usage is essential.

The Role of Education and Advocacy

Empowering personal action goes beyond individual choices—it also involves spreading knowledge, advocating for change, and mobilizing others. Education is a key catalyst for building collective action. When we educate ourselves about environmental issues, we become more informed advocates for the planet, and can help others understand the importance of sustainability.

Social media and community-based efforts can amplify our voices. Individuals have used platforms like Instagram, Twitter, and YouTube to spread messages about zero-waste living, ethical fashion, and climate activism, sparking wider movements. Activists like Greta Thunberg, who started with a solitary protest outside the Swedish parliament, have shown how powerful individual action can be in inspiring global change.

Additionally, local advocacy can create significant impact. Whether it's advocating for better waste management policies in your city, supporting local environmental organizations, or pushing for greener building codes and zoning laws, local action has the potential to influence change at the community level and beyond.

Empowering Youth and Future Generations

While the current generation holds substantial power in shaping the future, empowering youth is crucial for ensuring a sustainable legacy. Younger people are often more aware of the urgency of climate change and environmental degradation, and they are more likely to take bold action. Education systems can play a major role in this by integrating sustainability principles into school curriculums, offering practical courses on renewable energy, sustainable agriculture, and climate science.

Organizations like **Fridays for Future**, led by Greta Thunberg, have mobilized millions of young people around the world to demand climate action from governments and corporations. Youth movements have proven to be a powerful force for environmental change, challenging established political structures and demanding a future that prioritizes climate justice, clean energy, and biodiversity protection.

The power of individual action cannot be overstated. While it may seem that environmental change is beyond our control, personal choices have a significant cumulative effect on the world around us. By adopting more sustainable lifestyles, supporting ethical businesses, minimizing our carbon footprints, and advocating for systemic change, we can become catalysts for the movement toward a more sustainable, equitable world.

Personal action is not just about individual responsibility—it's about collective power. When millions of people make small changes, they become part of a larger movement that can shift industries, policies, and cultures. By empowering ourselves and those around us, we can turn the tide on the environmental crisis and pave the way for a brighter, greener future.

In the next section, we will explore how grassroots movements and community-based efforts are vital in creating change at the local level and influencing larger-scale environmental reform.

The Role of Grassroots Movements

While individual actions are vital, grassroots movements have long been a driving force in effecting social and political change. These movements, born from the ground up and often led by communities most affected by environmental degradation, are uniquely positioned to challenge existing power structures, mobilize people, and push for legislative and corporate reform. They highlight the profound impact of collective action and have been instrumental in raising awareness about critical environmental issues, from climate change to pollution to biodiversity loss.

What Are Grassroots Movements?

At their core, grassroots movements are community-driven efforts aimed at enacting change on a local, national, or even global scale. They rely on the involvement of ordinary people—often working outside of established political and corporate systems—to advocate for the common good. These movements usually emerge in response to a specific injustice or environmental issue, where individuals or communities feel that their voices are not being heard in traditional political forums. They aim to raise awareness, mobilize action, and influence policy by focusing on issues that directly affect people's lives.

In the context of environmental challenges, grassroots movements have played a crucial role in:

- **Raising public awareness** about issues like deforestation, pollution, and unsustainable farming.
- **Organizing campaigns and protests** to demand policy changes or corporate accountability.
- **Building local solutions** to environmental problems, such as community-driven recycling programs, sustainable agriculture initiatives, or clean energy projects.
- **Influencing policy at local, national, and global levels**, often by forming alliances with environmental organizations, activists, and sympathetic lawmakers.

These movements thrive on passion, persistence, and the belief that change is possible, even in the face of significant opposition. By building solidarity, mobilizing local resources, and amplifying their messages, grassroots groups can sometimes achieve extraordinary victories—disrupting the status quo and reshaping public discourse around environmental issues.

Examples of Powerful Grassroots Movements

1. **Fridays for Future**: Perhaps the most well-known contemporary grassroots movement, **Fridays for Future** was launched by Greta Thunberg in 2018. What started as a solitary protest outside the Swedish Parliament quickly morphed into a global youth movement, with millions of young people worldwide demanding that governments take urgent action to combat climate change. Thunberg's Fridays for Future has sparked mass demonstrations, lobbied for climate justice policies, and brought the issue of climate change to the forefront of global conversations. The movement has also pressured governments and institutions to adopt stricter climate goals in line with the **Paris Agreement**. **Impact:** The movement has achieved significant media attention and policy shifts, including pressure on governments to declare climate emergencies, pledge to reduce emissions, and implement green recovery packages post-pandemic. The movement is a powerful example of youth-led activism and how grassroots efforts can shake up global politics.

2. **The Standing Rock Sioux Tribe and the Dakota Access Pipeline**: In 2016, the Standing Rock Sioux Tribe in North Dakota led a historic protest against the construction of the Dakota Access Pipeline (DAPL), which they argued threatened the water supply for millions of people and violated Indigenous land rights. What began as a local issue soon grew into a global movement for Indigenous rights and environmental justice, attracting thousands of activists from around the world who gathered at the Standing Rock Reservation in solidarity. **Impact:** The movement successfully raised awareness about the dangers of fossil fuel extraction on Indigenous lands, highlighted the importance of protecting water resources, and spurred national conversations about environmental racism. While the pipeline was ultimately completed, the protests led to legal battles, public outcry, and a significant reevaluation of how pipelines and other major infrastructure projects are assessed and approved in the United States.

3. **Extinction Rebellion**: **Extinction Rebellion (XR)**, founded in 2018, is a global grassroots movement that uses nonviolent civil disobedience to demand urgent action on climate change and biodiversity loss. With its bold tactics, including blocking roads, occupying buildings, and organizing large-scale demonstrations, XR has brought climate emergency declarations to several cities and countries worldwide.

   Impact: The movement's slogan, **"Tell the Truth, Act Now, and Go Beyond Politics,"** has resonated with millions of people who feel the urgency of the climate crisis. Extinction Rebellion's direct actions have forced governments to respond, especially in countries like the UK, where XR has succeeded in pushing climate change to the top of the political agenda.

4.   **The Zero Waste Movement**: A decentralized, grassroots initiative that focuses on reducing waste, promoting recycling, and advocating for a circular economy, the **Zero Waste Movement** has been growing globally, particularly in urban centers. Originating in San Francisco in the 1990s, the movement promotes reducing waste to the point where only compostable materials remain. **Impact:** The Zero Waste movement has inspired cities around the world to adopt stricter waste reduction programs, build composting infrastructure, and push for corporate accountability in reducing single-use plastics. This movement has also brought attention to landfill overuse and its connection to climate change and pollution.

5.   **The Global Anti-Pollution Movement**: In response to increasing air and water pollution in cities across the globe, local communities have organized protests and campaigns against toxic industries, air pollution, and the dumping of chemicals into water supplies. Movements such as **#NoDAPL** (No Dakota Access Pipeline) and local air quality protests in India are examples of how grassroots groups push for cleaner environments and better regulatory oversight on industrial pollution. **Impact:** These grassroots actions have contributed to stronger environmental regulations, such as the **Clean Air Act** and **Clean Water Act** in the U.S., and have mobilized local communities to demand cleaner air, better waste management systems, and stricter environmental standards.

Grassroots Movements as Catalysts for Systemic Change

What makes grassroots movements so powerful is their ability to mobilize ordinary people and place issues on the political agenda that might otherwise be ignored by the powerful elites. By **engaging individuals at the local level and amplifying their voices through social media and collective action, these movements can break through the noise of traditional politics and force leaders to acknowledge the severity of environmental issues.**

Moreover, grassroots movements often lead to collaborative solutions that reflect the needs of those most affected. For example, **Indigenous-led movements** not only fight to protect their lands and cultures but also offer sustainable land management practices that can teach us how to live in harmony with nature. The **farm-to-table movements** and **community gardens** have reshaped how we think about food security and local economies, highlighting the need for food sovereignty and sustainable agriculture.

The urgency of the environmental crises means that these movements must grow, diversify, and strengthen. They must be recognized not as fringe protests but as central players in the fight for a sustainable future. Grassroots efforts can push governments, corporations, and global institutions to address the core issues that undermine environmental stability. But they also need our support.

Grassroots movements are proving that real change is possible when ordinary people come together with passion, purpose, and persistence. From protecting Indigenous lands to demanding urgent action on climate change, these movements are not only challenging the status quo but also creating new pathways to sustainability. By amplifying marginalized voices, building coalitions, and putting pressure on decision-makers, grassroots activism is paving the way for systemic reform and environmental justice.

As individuals, we can support these movements, **get involved in local campaigns,** and lend our voices to those fighting for a more sustainable, equitable world. In the next section, we will discuss how collective action, from local efforts to global mobilizations, has the power to influence policy changes and transform our environmental future.

Successful Examples of Collective Action

While individual actions and grassroots movements are crucial in driving change, the most powerful transformations occur when these efforts are united into broader collective actions. When communities, organizations, activists, and everyday people come together, they can create significant shifts in policy, industry practices, and public consciousness. Collective action amplifies the voices of individuals and can help move the needle on key environmental issues—transforming small, local victories into global wins.

1. The Paris Agreement and Global Climate Action

One of the most notable examples of collective action on a global scale is the adoption of the **Paris Agreement** in 2015. Following years of intense lobbying by climate activists, scientists, and a growing movement of concerned citizens worldwide, nearly every nation on Earth came together to sign an agreement aimed at limiting global warming to below 2°C, with an aspiration of 1.5°C. This agreement was the result of decades of grassroots campaigning, international advocacy, and the tireless efforts of individuals and communities who demanded that governments take bold action on climate change.

The agreement marked a significant victory for collective action, as it demonstrated that global environmental challenges require a united approach. It also showed that even though progress on climate change may seem slow and incremental at times, the combined efforts of nations, organizations, and individuals can produce meaningful outcomes. The Paris Agreement helped bring climate change to the forefront of political discussions worldwide and created a framework for future environmental collaboration.

Impact: The Paris Agreement led to major shifts in government policies and corporate strategies around the world. For example, many countries—especially in the European Union—committed to net-zero emissions goals, while companies in the renewable energy sector saw a surge in investment and innovation. The agreement also spurred new coalitions, such as the **We Are Still In** movement in the United States, which saw cities, states, and businesses coming together to honor the agreement even after the federal government withdrew from it in 2017.

2. The Divestment Movement: Taking Money Out of Fossil Fuels

The divestment movement is another example of powerful collective action that has forced the hand of fossil fuel companies and brought greater attention to the climate crisis. This movement encourages individuals, institutions, and governments to divest from fossil fuel industries—**selling off investments in coal, oil, and gas companies—and redirect that capital into renewable energy or other sustainable initiatives.**

The movement began on college campuses in the early 2010s, with **students calling on their universities to remove fossil fuel investments from their endowments.** What started as a small campaign soon turned into a global movement, with financial institutions, pension funds, and even city governments pledging to divest from fossil fuels. The Fossil Free Index reports that over $14 trillion in assets have been divested as of 2023, with more institutions joining the movement every year.

Impact: The divestment movement has had a profound effect on the fossil fuel industry. By making it more difficult for these companies to secure capital, divestment is raising the costs of doing business in fossil fuels and increasing pressure for companies to transition to cleaner energy. In turn, it has sparked new investments in renewable energy and green technologies, helping to shift the financial system away from fossil fuel dependency.

3. The Plastic Pollution Crisis: Bans and Boycotts

Plastic pollution is one of the most pressing environmental issues today, with millions of tons of plastic waste ending up in our oceans every year. Collective action, both at the grassroots and global level, has been instrumental in challenging the plastic industry and pushing for systemic change.

For instance, in 2018, the **#BreakFreeFromPlastic** movement gained traction as citizens, NGOs, and local governments took action to tackle the growing plastic waste problem. The campaign led to a series of successful plastic bans, including the plastic straw ban in the UK, and national policies in several countries to restrict plastic bags and single-use plastics.

Impact: The movement also influenced major corporations to adopt more sustainable practices. In response to the mounting pressure, companies like Nestlé, Coca-Cola, and Unilever pledged to reduce plastic packaging and invest in circular economy initiatives. Meanwhile, cities like San Francisco, Mumbai, and Bangkok implemented bold policies that drastically reduced plastic waste in their communities.

Moreover, consumer boycotts of plastic-heavy brands and products have forced companies to reconsider their packaging strategies, while local initiatives have created new models for zero-waste cities. The momentum from these collective actions has sparked a growing global movement to hold companies and governments accountable for their role in plastic pollution.

4. The Rise of Renewable Energy Cooperatives

Another remarkable example of collective action can be found in the global rise of community-based renewable energy projects. In many parts of the world, citizens are coming together to invest in local solar and wind energy projects, allowing them to take control of their energy needs and reduce their reliance on fossil fuels.

In Germany, the Energiewende (Energy Transition) movement has led to the establishment of thousands of community-owned renewable energy cooperatives that contribute to the country's goal of achieving 100% renewable energy by 2050. These cooperatives allow local residents to invest in wind farms, solar arrays, and other clean energy technologies, while keeping the financial benefits within their communities.

Impact: Renewable energy cooperatives are helping democratize energy production, ensuring that communities—rather than corporate giants—have the power to decide how their energy is generated and consumed. This model not only reduces carbon emissions but also builds local economies and creates jobs in the renewable energy sector. It's a clear example of how collective action can pave the way for a cleaner, more equitable energy future.

5. Global Movements for Climate Justice

The fight for climate justice is another example of the power of collective action in addressing the intersection of environmental and social inequalities. Movements such as 350.org, Fridays for Future, and the Sunrise Movement in the U.S. have centered their campaigns on the importance of addressing climate change in ways that are just, equitable, and inclusive. These movements emphasize that the people who are most vulnerable to the impacts of climate change—such as Indigenous communities, low-income populations, and communities of color—are often the least responsible for causing it.

Impact: The push for climate justice has resulted in numerous policy victories, including the creation of climate reparations funds, just transition policies, and commitments from governments to support the most vulnerable communities through climate adaptation and resilience measures. Additionally, it has helped reshape the global conversation about climate action, making it clear that sustainability is not only an environmental issue but a human rights issue as well.

Collective action is the backbone of transformative change in the fight for a sustainable future. From global agreements like the Paris Agreement to local movements pushing for renewable energy and plastic bans, people working together have shown time and again that united efforts can overcome powerful forces. These movements, whether fueled by youth activism, community-based initiatives, or widespread public pressure, remind us that when individuals stand together, they can change policies, industries, and the course of history.

The successes of collective action demonstrate that real, lasting change is possible. But these victories are only the beginning. We must continue to support and amplify grassroots movements, unite across borders, and hold ourselves and our leaders accountable for the future we wish to see. The environmental challenges we face may seem overwhelming, but they are not insurmountable. When we work together, we have the power to shape a sustainable, just world for generations to come.

As we close this chapter, it is essential to remember that while individual efforts are crucial, it is only through collective will and solidarity that we can achieve lasting change. Together, we can build a movement powerful enough to protect our planet—and the future of life on Earth.

A Call To Action
Our Responsibility to Future Generations

The environmental crises we face today are not isolated events but a series of interconnected challenges that affect every corner of our planet. From climate change to biodiversity loss, from pollution to water scarcity, these issues are not just a threat to the natural world—they are a threat to our collective well-being and the survival of future generations. But amid these daunting challenges, there is a growing recognition that the solutions lie not in small, incremental changes, but in a global movement toward sustainability.

The term "sustainability" has become a buzzword in recent years, but it is much more than a trend or a catchphrase. At its heart, sustainability is about ensuring that our actions today do not undermine the ability of future generations to meet their needs. It's about shifting our entire way of life—from how we produce and consume energy to how we grow our food, manage our waste, and interact with the natural world. Sustainability is not just an environmental issue; it is a social, economic, and cultural one, requiring a fundamental rethinking of how we live on this planet.

Across the globe, we are already witnessing the beginnings of such a movement. From the streets of Stockholm to the villages of Bangladesh, from urban centers in Germany to the rural landscapes of Brazil, people are coming together to demand change. These efforts are not just led by governments or corporations; they are grassroots movements, powered by communities, activists, students, and everyday citizens. They are individuals and organizations fighting for clean energy, sustainable food systems, climate justice, and environmental protection.

The growing climate strikes organized by youth around the world, the calls for green new deals in governments, the rise of eco-conscious consumerism, and the shifts in corporate responsibility are all part of a larger, global awakening. What we are witnessing is a critical moment in human history—a movement that could transform our societies and economies into something more just, equitable, and sustainable. The question is not whether this change will come, but whether we, as a global community, will have the courage and determination to make it happen before it is too late.

This movement is already gaining momentum, but it needs to continue to grow. It needs every single one of us to get involved. Whether it's through our individual actions, supporting local initiatives, or pushing for larger systemic changes, we all have a role to play. From young people taking to the streets to world leaders forging international agreements, every action counts. The future of the planet is in our hands, and it is clear that the power of collective action—through local, national, and international movements—will shape the course of history.

The transition to a sustainable future is not easy, nor will it be quick. The forces that have led to environmental degradation—corporate greed, political inertia, and unsustainable growth models—are entrenched. But history is on the side of those who demand change. When people unite for a common cause, they can shift the course of history. It is time to unite in a shared vision of a sustainable, just world for all. This is the movement we need to build and sustain—a global movement toward sustainability.

Our Responsibility to Future Generations

As we reflect on the pressing environmental challenges we face, one fundamental truth stands clear: **the choices we make today will determine the future of the planet and all who inhabit it**. The environmental degradation we are witnessing—whether in the form of rising temperatures, melting ice caps, biodiversity loss, or pollution—is not just an abstract concept or a problem for future generations to solve. It is our responsibility to take decisive action now to preserve the planet for those who come after us.

This is not simply a matter of protecting the environment for its own sake, but for the sake of the millions of people—especially the most vulnerable—who depend on a stable and thriving planet for their survival. Climate change, for example, has already begun to displace entire communities, exacerbating poverty, triggering migrations, and causing devastating impacts on public health. We see this most acutely in low-income countries, where communities that have contributed the least to the problem are suffering the most. The urgency of addressing these crises is not just an environmental issue; it is a matter of justice.

The idea of intergenerational responsibility—of leaving behind a livable planet for our children and grandchildren—is one of the core principles of sustainability. But this responsibility goes beyond merely preserving resources or reducing emissions. It is about creating systems and structures that are just, equitable, and resilient, ensuring that future generations not only inherit a healthy planet but also have the opportunity to thrive. This is a responsibility we must take seriously.

We are the stewards of this Earth. It is we who must reconcile our economic models with the realities of the environment. It is we who must demand that corporations be held accountable, that governments create policies that protect rather than exploit, and that our society as a whole shifts toward a more equitable, sustainable future. In this light, the actions we take now—no matter how small they may seem—are inextricably linked to the quality of life future generations will inherit.

But responsibility to future generations goes beyond just the physical health of the planet—it also involves preserving a sense of hope and possibility. Imagine a world where our children inherit a thriving, biodiverse planet, where clean air and water are the norm, where renewable energy powers homes and industries, and where healthy, sustainable food systems nourish all people. Imagine a world where social justice and environmental justice go hand in hand, where the most marginalized communities have the resources and support they need to thrive in the face of climate change. This is the kind of world we must work toward—a world we can be proud to pass on.

At the same time, we must confront the uncomfortable reality that our generation will be judged by the legacy we leave behind. Will we be remembered as the generation that failed to act in the face of overwhelming evidence? Or will we be remembered as the generation that rose to the occasion, that recognized the urgency of the crisis and took meaningful, bold steps to protect the planet?

This is the challenge we face: to act with the long-term interests of humanity at the forefront of our decisions. The path to a sustainable future will not be easy. It will require sacrifices, difficult decisions, and a willingness to challenge the status quo. But it is the only path forward if we are to leave the world in a better place than we found it.

Our children, and their children after them, will inherit the world we create today. We owe it to them to ensure that world is one of opportunity, resilience, and **hope**, not a broken and degraded environment that they must struggle to repair. Our actions, no matter how small or large, will echo through time, influencing the future trajectory of life on Earth.

We have the power. We have the knowledge. Now, it is time to take responsibility.

The urgency of the environmental crises we face cannot be overstated. Climate change, deforestation, biodiversity loss, and pollution are not distant threats—they are here, now, and they are escalating. The time for action is today, and it is our responsibility to future generations to take that action seriously. We must rise to the challenge, unite in our efforts, and take bold, decisive steps to build a sustainable future.

The choices we make today will shape the world of tomorrow. We have the power to create a better world for our children, one that is just, equitable, and sustainable. But we cannot wait. The actions we take now will define the legacy we leave behind. Our responsibility to future generations is clear: act now, and act with urgency, for the sake of the planet, its ecosystems, and the future of humanity. Let us rise to this moment and be the generation that secures a sustainable, thriving future for all who come after us.

A Hopeful, Empowering Message

While the challenges ahead may seem overwhelming, there is an undeniable power in hope—and more importantly, in action. The truth is that the solutions to our environmental crises already exist. They are being implemented in pockets around the world, tested in small communities, and championed by passionate individuals and organizations. What we need now is to scale these solutions, to harness the momentum that is building, and to recognize that every one of us has the power to make a difference.

Hope is not passive. It is the belief that change is possible, followed by the courage to take the first step toward that change. This is the type of hope we must nurture. It's the kind that comes from seeing that small efforts accumulate, that collective action can overturn entrenched systems, and that when we work together—whether as individuals, communities, or nations—we can turn the tide. The journey toward sustainability is long, but it is not hopeless. Every change, no matter how small, is a victory on the path to a better future.

Consider the extraordinary momentum of movements like **Fridays for Future**, led by young climate activists like Greta Thunberg, whose message has inspired millions to demand urgent climate action from governments and industries. Or look to the rise of renewable energy cooperatives and the global shift toward plant-based diets, showing that communities and individuals can choose sustainability. Even corporate commitments to reducing carbon footprints, while imperfect, demonstrate that market forces are beginning to align with the need for change.

These efforts show that we are not powerless. **Change is happening**, and it is happening at a pace faster than many might realize. We do not have to wait for a perfect solution or for every problem to be fixed before we begin. What matters is that we **take action**—in our personal lives, in our communities, and in our broader movements—and push for the policies, practices, and systems that will ensure a sustainable future.

But this hope is not blind optimism. It's grounded in reality—the reality that we already have the knowledge, the tools, and the creativity to build a sustainable world. The question is no longer "Can we?" but "Will we?" Will we rise to meet the challenge? Will we make the changes required? **The future of the planet is in our hands**, and while the stakes are higher than ever, the potential for positive change is greater than ever before. We are the ones we have been waiting for.

As we close this book, let's be clear: **the fight for a sustainable future is not over—it's just beginning**. We have witnessed the urgency of our environmental crises and the deep, systemic issues holding us back from meaningful progress. But we also know this: **the power to change is within our reach**. It lies in our hands, in our voices, and in our actions.

This is not a time to despair, but a time to act. We must take responsibility—for ourselves, for our communities, and for the generations that will follow. The future will be shaped by the choices we make today, and it is not too late to make the difference needed.

Each step we take, whether big or small, brings us closer to the future we want—a world that thrives on justice, sustainability, and equity. A future where clean energy, sustainable food systems, and healthy ecosystems are the norm. A future where people live in harmony with nature, not in conflict with it.

The call to action is clear. The path is challenging, but the rewards are immeasurable. Together, we have the power to create a world where future generations can live, flourish, and thrive. Let's seize that power. Let's act now, let's act with urgency, and let's do it together—because our planet needs us, and future generations are counting on us.

The work begins today. And it begins with **each one of us**.

We are the change.

9 798305 284539